Bread & Wine is one of those rare books that grabs all of you—your mind, body, and spirit. Shauna's soulful storytelling made me laugh, reminded me that I'm not alone, and gave me a new lens on some old struggles. There's something sacred about this kind of truth telling. I couldn't put this book down.

> **Brené Brown,** PhD, *New York Times* bestselling author of *Daring Greatly: How the Courage to be Vulnerable Transforms the Way We Live, Love, Parent and Lead*

Bread & Wine is a new book about an ancient meal, but more than a meal, a book about the people seated at the table, and about the laughing, and about the joy of saying hello and the pain of saying good-bye. After reading this book you may feel as you do driving away from dinner with a friend—grateful and full.

> **Donald Miller,** author of *Blue Like Jazz* and *A Million Miles in a Thousand Years*

Shauna Niequist's beautiful word painting in *Bread & Wine* is a poetic reminder to appreciate the rituals, people, and sensory experiences of our everyday lives. Her words invite us into her kitchen, and her stories challenge us to remain attentive to the many delights that complement life's hardships and the ways in which we can share them with others.

> **Kelle Hampton,** *New York Times* bestselling author of *Bloom: Finding Beauty in the Unexpected*

No one combines all my treasured things like Shauna does in *Bread & Wine*: beautiful words, delicious food, recipes like the ones you jot down on the back of a napkin in shorthand, with hints and adaptations written off to the side, real-life stories, laughter. Then I read a sentence like this: "Love isn't something you prove or earn, but something you receive or allow, like a balm, like a benediction, even at your very worst," and I decide to send this book to everyone I know.

> **Jen Hatmaker,** author of *Interrupted* and *7: An Experimental Mutiny Against Excess*

This magnificent book is a feast for the soul! A wise, thoughtful, and delightful read that will nourish your heart.

> **Ian Morgan Cron,** bestselling author of *Jesus, My Father, the CIA, and Me: a Memoir ... of Sorts* and *Chasing Francis*

Bread & Wine resurrects the table as the center of the home, the place where food and drink morph into fellowship and long memories. This book transported me back to the kitchens of my life—to the fellowship and joy and sorrow of what happens when the family gathers around the table to be family. Churches need books about kitchen tables because they value the home and family and the treasured memories of family stories told at the table.

> **Scot McKnight,** Northern Seminary, author of *The King Jesus Gospel*

Bam! Yummo! This is a tasty and delicious book you'll want to savor from cover to cover.

> **Margaret Feinberg** (www.margaretfeinberg.com), author of *Wonderstruck* and *Scouting the Divine*

Shauna Niequist has a way with words that makes you feel more human, more alive. Every phrase is woven together in a way that inspires wonder at the most ordinary of events we are prone to pass by. This book will make you hungry—not just for food, but for life and love to the full. It certainly did for me.

> **Jeff Goins,** author of *Wrecked: When a Broken World Slams into Your Comfortable Life*

Shauna Niequist has written a book of surpassing delight. To enter it is not simply to be a reader but to be a friend. I did not want it to end.

> **John Ortberg,** senior pastor of Menlo Park Presbyterian Church and author of *Who Is This Man?*

Bread & Wine

a love letter
to life around the table,
with recipes

shauna niequist

ZONDERVAN®

ZONDERVAN.com/
AUTHORTRACKER
follow your favorite authors

ZONDERVAN

Bread & Wine
Copyright © 2013 by Shauna Niequist

This title is also available as a Zondervan ebook. Visit www.zondervan.com/ebooks.

This title is also available in a Zondervan audio edition. Visit www.zondervan.fm.

Requests for information should be addressed to:
Zondervan, *Grand Rapids, Michigan 49530*

ISBN 978-0-310-32817-9

Published in association with ChristopherFerebee.com, attorney and literary agent.

Cover design: Michelle Lenger
Cover photograpy: Johner / Glasshouse Images
Cover and interior calligraphy: Lindsay Sherbondy
Interior design: Beth Shagene

Printed in the United States of America

13 14 15 16 17 18 19 /DCI/ 22 21 20 19 18 17 16 15 14 13 12 11 10 9 8 7 6

For my boys —
Aaron, Henry, and Mac

And for the Cooking Club —
Brannon Anderson
Margaret Hogan
Amanda Hybels
Melody Martinez
Casey Sundstedt

contents

part three

part four

appendix

author's note

I'm not a recipe writer, for the most part. Many of these recipes—favorites around our table—are from chefs, cookbook writers, and restaurants I love, and I'm so happy to pass them on to you. At the beginning of each recipe, I've noted the source or inspiration, and I hope you buy the cookbooks, read the magazines, or bookmark the blogs, and that you find as much inspiration and instruction in them as I have.

In many cases, I've adapted these recipes for simplicity or preference along the way. They are, like all recipes, intended to be tinkered with and made your own, according to your tastes and your story, according to your family and your table.

Many of the recipes are gluten-free, and several of those recipes include oats. Some people who eat gluten-free, like my husband, Aaron, have no trouble with oats. For others, and certainly for people with celiac disease, only certified gluten-free oats will do.

Also on the topic of gluten-free cooking, some of these recipes call for almond meal. Almond meal can be made in a food processor by whizzing up raw almonds till they become fine like sand, but before you end up with almond butter. Or you can buy it at health food stores and Trader Joe's.

A few more things: the only salt I use is sea salt, and I always use salted butter. Every recipe is made to serve 6 people, unless otherwise specified. I generally make the full recipe for our little family because I love a serving or two of leftovers the next day; for a dinner party of 10 to 12 people, I double the recipe.

My prayer is that you'll read these pages first curled up on your couch or in bed or in the bathtub, and then after that you'll bring it to the kitchen with you, turning corners of pages, breaking the spine, spilling red wine on it, and splashing vinegar across the pages, that it will become battered and stained as you cook and chop and play, music loud and kitchen messy.

And more than anything, I pray that when you put this book down, you'll gather the people you love around your table to eat and drink, to tell stories, to be heard and fed and nourished on every level.

on bread and wine

I'm a bread person—crusty, golden baguette; hearty, grainy, seeded loaves; thin, crispy pizza crust—all of it. Flaky, buttery croissants; chewy pita; tortillas, warm and fragrant, blistered by heat. Whenever my jeans are too tight, I'm reminded that I know better than to love bread the way I do, but love is blind, and certainly beyond reason. And I am a wine person—the blood-red and liquid gold, the clink and glamour of tall-stemmed glasses, and the musty, rich, almost mushroom-y smell.

More than that, I am a bread-and-wine person. By that I mean that I'm a Christian, a person of the body and blood, a person of the bread and wine. Like every Christian, I recognize the two as food and drink, and also, at the very same time, I recognize them as something much greater—mystery and tradition and symbol. Bread is bread, and wine is wine, but bread-and-wine is another thing entirely. The two together are the sacred and the material at once, the heaven and earth, the divine and the daily.

This is a collection of essays about family, friendships, and the meals that bring us together. It's about the ways God teaches and nourishes us as we nourish the people around us, and about hunger, both physical and otherwise, and the connections between the two.

It's about food and family and faith. It's also about everything else, because all of life is a jumble of ideas and experiences and the things we find under the couch cushions. All of life is a whirling mash-up of the big and little things—the things we see and think and remember and smell and feel, the deep values that guide us and the dirt under our fingernails, the undercurrents of belief and doubt and the coolness of cotton sheets right when we slide our toes down to the bottom of the bed. It's about food, and it's not. It's about life, which is to say it's about everything.

A few Christmases ago, my dear friends Steve and Sarah gave me a book called *My Last Supper*. It's a gorgeous, oversized hardcover with a collection of interviews with fifty great chefs about their last suppers. Apparently that's one of those age-old kitchen questions chefs and cooks discuss ad infinitum, in lulls between service, as they close down the kitchen at the end of a busy night—*If you knew it was your very last meal, what would you eat? Who would cook it? What would you drink, who would be around the table with you, if you knew it was your very last meal?*

Being married to a musician, I'm very familiar with the musician's equivalent: *Out of all recorded music, what song do you wish you had written?* Or *If you were putting together your dream band, who would play each instrument?* For an English major like me, it's something like, *If you could sit in a café with one writer, who would you choose?* Or maybe, *What line do you wish you had written?* It's one of those questions you can discuss forever, and change your answer a little bit every time, one that you love answering, because it permits you to live in that world—the food world, the music world, the literary world—for as long as you're working out your answer. If you're like me, you keep changing your answer, because you want to stay in that world for as long as possible.

For the record, my last-supper meal looks a bit like this: first, of course, ice-cold champagne, gallons of it, flutes catching the candlelight and dancing. There would be bacon-wrapped dates oozing with goat cheese, and risotto with thick curls of Parmesan and flecks of black pepper. There would be paper-thin pizza with tomatoes and mozzarella and slim ribbons of basil, garlicky pasta and crusty bread and lots of cheeses, a plummy pinot noir and maybe a really dirty martini, because you might as well go big on your last night on earth. There would be dark chocolate sea salted toffee and a bowl of fat blackberries, and we'd stay at the table for hours and hours, laughing and telling stories and reaching for one more bite, one more bite, one more bite.

What's becoming clearer and clearer to me is that the most sacred moments, the ones in which I feel God's presence most profoundly, when I feel the goodness of the world most arrestingly, take place at the table. The particular alchemy of celebration and food, of connecting people and serving what I've made with my own hands, comes together as more than the sum of their parts. I love the sounds and smells and textures of life at the table, hands passing bowls and forks clinking against plates and bread being torn and the rhythm and energy of feeding and being fed.

I love to talk about food and cooking and entertaining. I want to hear about how other people do it, and about the surprising and significant things that happen when people gather around the table. Many of the books I've read and loved most dearly have been about food and gatherings at the table. My best moments have been spent in the kitchen, and many of the most deeply spiritual moments of the last year have taken place at the table.

It's not, actually, strictly, about food for me. It's about what happens when we come together, slow down, open our homes, look into one another's faces, listen to one another's stories. It happens when we leave the office and get a sitter and skip our workouts every so often to celebrate a birthday or an accomplishment or a wedding or a birth, when we break out of the normal clockwork of daily life and pop the champagne on a cold, gray Wednesday for no other reason than the fact that the faces we love are gathered around our table. It happens when we enter the joy and the sorrow of the people we love, and we join together at the table to feed one another and be fed, and while it's not strictly about food, it doesn't happen without it. Food is the starting point, the common ground, the thing to hold and handle, the currency we offer to one another.

It's no accident that when a loved one dies, the family is deluged with food. The impulse to feed is innate. Food is a language of care, the thing we do when traditional language fails us, when we don't know what to say, when there are no words to say. And food is what we offer in celebration—at weddings, at anniversaries, at happy events of every kind. It's the thing that connects us, that bears our traditions, our sense of home and family, our deepest memories, and, on a practical level, our ability to live and breathe each day. Food matters.

At the very beginning, and all through the Bible, all through the stories about God and his people, there are stories about food, about all of life changing with the bite of an apple, about trading an inheritance for a bowl of stew, about waking up to find the land littered with bread, God's way of caring for his people; about a wedding where water turned to wine, Jesus' first miracle; about the very first Last Supper, the humble bread and wine becoming, for all time, indelibly linked to the very body of Christ, the center point for thousands of years of tradition and belief. It matters. It mattered then, and it matters now, possibly even more so, because it's a way of reclaiming some of the things we may have lost along the way.

Both the church and modern life, together and separately, have wandered away from the table. The church has preferred to live in the mind and the heart and the soul, and almost not at all in fingers and mouths and senses. And modern life has pushed us into faux food and fast food and highly engineered food products cased in sterile packages that we eat in the car or on the subway— as though we're astronauts, as though we can't be bothered with a meal.

What happens around the table doesn't matter to a lot of people. But it matters more and more to me. Life at the table is life at its best to me, and the spiritual significance of what and how we eat, and with whom and where, is new and profound to me every day. I believe God is here among us, present and working. I believe all of life is shot through with God's presence, and that part of the gift of walking with him is seeing his fingerprints in all sorts of unexpected ways.

My friend Nancy is a nature person. To know her is to know that the created world—mountains, wildflowers, sunshine—is the tie that binds her to God, that demonstrates his presence to her in the deepest ways. For my dad, it's the water. The sounds and smells and rituals of life on the water bind him to God in ways that nothing else does. For my husband, Aaron, it's music. And for me, it's the table.

What makes me feel alive and connected to God's voice and spirit in this world is creating opportunities for the people I love to rest and connect and be fed at my table. I believe it's the way I was made, and I believe it matters. For many years, I didn't let it matter, for a whole constellation of reasons, but part of becoming yourself, in a deeply spiritual way, is finding the words to tell the truth about what it is you really love. In the words of my favorite poet, Mary Oliver, it's about "letting the soft animal of your body love what it loves."

My friends and I didn't learn to cook, necessarily. In an effort to widen our options, to set us free to be whatever we wanted to be, many of our mothers shooed us out of the kitchen—that place of lingering oppression and captivity for many of them.

They encouraged us to study and travel and participate in sports and the arts, the things women didn't get to do when they were young. They shooed us out as an act of love, regardless of the fact that some of us really wanted to be there. So then, largely, young women and men moved out of their parents' homes and didn't know how to cook at all, and both genders felt conflicted about it, for a host of reasons. So we got takeout and thought about other things.

But many of us, men and women alike, at a certain point, are wandering back to the kitchen and fumbling and learning and trying to feed ourselves and the people we love, because we sense that it's important and that we may have missed something fundamental along the way. Especially for those of us who make our livings largely in front of computer screens, there's something extraordinary about getting up from the keyboard and using our hands for something besides typing—for chopping and dicing and coaxing scents and flavors from the raw materials in front of us. There's something entirely satisfying in a modern, increasingly virtual world about something so elemental—heat, knife, sizzle.

The cookbooks and food writing I enjoy most are written by people who love to eat, people who are not above what I would call regular-people food. Tell me you eat toast. Tell me you love cheap candy or fake cheese (I, for one, deeply love fake cheese). Tell me that every so often you find yourself standing over the sink eating leftovers, and that they're running down your chin. I know there are people who see food primarily as calories, nutrients, complex bundles of energy for the whirring machines of our bodies. I know them, but they're not my people. They're in the same general category of people who wear sensible shoes and read manuals. Good people, but entirely foreign to me.

I'm not a cook, and this isn't a cookbook. I have no illusions of opening a fine-dining fusion restaurant or a charming bed-and-breakfast, wearing an apron and making scones every morning. My husband will tell you we eat plenty of takeout and that I have a truly manic commitment to leftovers. I'll eat the same thing eight meals in a row, just so it doesn't go to waste.

I'm not a stickler about nutrition or a purist about organics, although I care about those things. I'm learning about them little by little, and living them step by step, meal by meal. I'm not a vegan and I don't eat low-carb, and I don't want you to change the way you eat, necessarily. But I do want you to love what you eat, and to share food with people you love, and to gather people together, for frozen pizza or filet mignon, because I think the gathering is of great significance.

When you eat, I want you to think of God, of the holiness of hands that feed us, of the provision we are given every time we eat. When you eat bread and you drink wine, I want you to think about the body and the blood every time, not just when the bread and wine show up in church, but when they show up anywhere — on a picnic table or a hardwood floor or a beach.

Some of my most sacred meals have been eaten out of travel mugs on camping trips or on benches on the street in Europe. Many of them have been at our own table or around our coffee table, leaning back against the couch. They've been high food and low food, fresh and frozen, extravagant and right out of the pizza box. It's about the table, and about all the other places we find ourselves eating. It's about a spirit or quality of living that rises up when we offer one another life itself, in the form of dinner or soup or breakfast, or bread and wine.

part one

"When you wake up in the morning, Pooh," said Piglet at last, "what's the first thing you say to yourself?"

"What's for breakfast?" said Pooh. "What do *you* say, Piglet?"

"I say, I wonder what's going to happen exciting *today*?" said Piglet.

Pooh nodded thoughtfully.

"It's the same thing," he said.

A. A. MILNE, *Winnie-the-Pooh*

my mom's blueberry crisp

My mom's dad is Irish, a storyteller and twinkling-eyed joker, and her mom is German, a rose gardener and meticulous baker. They met in the third grade in Vicksburg, Michigan. My grandpa's family moved away at the end of that school year, but my grandparents reconnected at the end of high school, and my grandpa insists he remembered her beautiful face all those years. They were married just before my grandpa joined the navy, and my mom, their first child, was born at Pearl Harbor.

Neither one of them grew up in religious homes, but when they married, they decided that religion was important and that they wanted to join a church. They visited all sorts of churches before settling at Lake Center Bible Church. Over the years they were members at other Bible churches for a few seasons, but these days they're active members and volunteers at Lake Center once again, almost sixty years later.

My dad's family is 100 percent Dutch, and they built a large produce company in Kalamazoo, Michigan. They owned farms all over the world, and a warehouse, and their trucks delivered produce to stores, restaurants, and hotels all over the country. My dad and his siblings all worked at the warehouse or in the fields or driving trucks. When each child turned five years old, they began spending Saturdays at the warehouse with little wagons, moving produce around, filling orders.

They were faithful members of a Christian Reformed church in Kalamazoo, a church that was strict and orderly, that emphasized observance of the Sabbath and thriftiness and looked down on frivolity and high emotion.

They were meat-and-potatoes people, men who worked long days on the farm and ate accordingly. Some days the farm lunch was a loaf of white bread and a pound of bologna per person. They'd fry the bologna in a frying pan with butter and make a tall stack of sandwiches for each of them.

And then six brothers—my grandfather and my dad's five uncles—all died of heart attacks before they were fifty-five. When I was born, my parents knew something had to change, that my dad had inherited those same dangerous genetics, and that nutrition was a way to stand up to what seemed terrifying and inevitable.

My mom was enamored, like all new moms are, with how perfect and pure her new baby was. She only wanted to feed me things that were healthy and whole. Because of that, and because of my dad's scary family health history, my mother became a health food person way before it was fashionable.

When other kids were eating Froot Loops in whole milk and Twinkies and Little Debbie snack cakes, my mom fed my younger brother and me whole grains, tofu, and skim milk. We ate almost no processed foods and very little red meat, and we never had "junk food"—soda, chips, store-bought cookies—in our home. While our friends were having hamburgers and sloppy joes on soft white buns, we were eating tuna over whole grain pasta and lentil burgers and muesli.

This was a time and place—the suburbs of Chicago in the early 1980s—when yogurt was weird and hummus was downright horrifying. In my school lunch, I had whole grain bread, all-fruit preserves, and the kind of peanut butter that had been ground from peanuts at the health food store, a place that smelled like vitamins and mulch. I also had a massive bag of carrots and sometimes an apricot fruit leather, which is just as luscious as it sounds. Why would anyone ever want to eat something whose greatest selling point is its textural similarity to leather?

These were the days when trading at lunch was a major feature of social politics, and I was deeply embarrassed about my lunch. I longed for white bread, American cheese, Cheetos, Hawaiian Punch. This was before Whole Foods and Trader Joe's and farmers markets with live music and cute, scruffy organic farmers peddling kale. This was when health food stores, tofu, and lentils were all vaguely suspect, and not at all upscale and respectable. Now half my friends get CSA boxes and many of our playdates involve the farmers market. Our friends and family are an assortment of gluten-free, dairy-free, vegetarian, vegan. Whole grains and quinoa are ubiquitous. Back then, though, this kind of stuff made you weird.

Exhibit A: the year my mom handed out mini-toothbrushes on Halloween, feeling that after all that sugar, a good brush would be thoughtful. Seriously? I was already hanging by a thread socially. I was already a pastor's kid, which is uncool on a thousand different levels. I already had a weird, organic, all-brown lunch. Now we're the toothbrush-on-Halloween family? Mom, you're killing me.

Now that I'm an adult, I appreciate how much effort this must have entailed, how expensive it was, how loving it was for her to feed us in that way. But as a child, all I knew was that my lunches were weird and that my cousins didn't want to sleep over at our house unless they could bring their own breakfast because they were absolutely terrified about what might turn up on their plates at our house. My cousin Melody always packed her own cinnamon-raisin bagel because she didn't want to risk Grape-Nuts or whole wheat pancakes for breakfast.

My parents and their friends started a church the year I was born, and part of being a church family means that your weekly calendar runs on a different rhythm than other families'. Sunday mornings were workdays, and often Saturdays too, so the weekend really began for us on Sundays after church.

After we got home from the early service, my mom and my brother and I would wait to hear my dad's heavy footsteps coming down the long, tiled hallway after the last service. He always went straight to his closet to change from his church clothes into his Chicago Bears sweatshirt, and when he walked through the study door, the weekend began. He was tired but happy, loose, easygoing.

Sunday afternoons were family time—private, casual, silly. We got to watch the Bears game while we did our homework in the study instead of doing it at the kitchen table like we usually did. My mom made sushi for lunch, and for dinner, blueberry crisp.

My mom baked her blueberry crisp in a round, blue earthenware baking dish, deep enough for there to be several inches of warm, bursting berries under the sweetness of the crisp topping. The dish had a fitted lid and handles on each side, and she would bring it down to the study with potholders and with the lid on, so that even if we had seconds, it was still warm.

She topped each bowl of crisp with a scoop of Breyers vanilla bean ice cream, flecked with dark specks of vanilla, and the ice cream melted into the crisp layer and the hot berries in thick, creamy rivers. Those Sunday nights were some of the only times we had ice cream at home, a special treat. More than that, it was a treat to taste summertime in the middle of winter, to taste the flavors of the lake back at home in the suburbs.

Since my brother, Todd, and I were little, our family spent every summer in South Haven, Michigan, on the shores of Lake Michigan. South Haven is a beach town an hour from where my parents grew up. My dad's parents had a cottage there, and both my grandfathers had sailboats in the marina. It's the town where my parents had their first date, and the setting for most of our family's richest memories.

South Haven is the blueberry capital of the country, and at the end of the summer every year we'd bring home bags and bags of blueberries to freeze. I remember getting home from the lake just in time for school to start, and while we unpacked and sorted sandy towels to wash, my mom covered the kitchen counters with towels, picked through the berries, washed and sorted them, and packed them into freezer bags so that all year long we could have blueberry crisp on Sunday nights in the study.

And now Aaron and I spend our summers in that same town. Henry swims on the same stretch of beach that Todd and I did, that my dad and his siblings did. We take the boat up and down the river that both my grandfathers sailed on all those years ago.

My mom keeps a small shelf of cookbooks at the cottage, and I reread them over and over every summer, lazily, almost from memory. My favorite is a small book the size of a paperback novel, called *Keeping Entertaining Simple* by Martha Storey. On the topic of fruit crisps, she recommends that you premeasure the fruit and freeze it in individual bags, and also that you make up a large batch of crisp topping and freeze it in individual bags too, one bag containing enough topping for one pan of crisp.

When we came back from the lake this year, on our way out of town we stopped at Barden's Farm Stand so I could buy twenty pounds of blueberries and a peck of peaches. When we got home, while I should have been unpacking and sorting laundry, I instead washed, dried, and sorted all those blueberries and then measured them into individual bags, each one with the perfect amount for one pan of crisp. Then I measured out batches of crisp topping and froze that too. And now we have blueberry crisp at the ready all year long, perfect for cozy Sunday nights, just like my mom had all those years ago.

Blueberry Crisp

There are all sorts of ways to make a fruit crisp, and most recipes are some version of flour, sugar, butter, oats, and cinnamon, but I asked myself: What would my mother do? This crisp is definitely her style—healthy and lightly sweet, fresh and simple.

I wanted something without flour so that Aaron, who eats gluten-free, could eat it, and I wanted to avoid sugar and butter if possible so that I could eat it for breakfast and feel virtuous. After a summer of doughnuts and cobbler and croissants for breakfast, I need a little virtue.

I've landed on this maple pecan version that's great with both blueberries and peaches, and a combination of the two is fantastic. I bet it would be lovely with apples or pears too—we'll try that this fall.

Some fruit crisp recipes call for cornstarch, lemon, or sugar mixed in with the fruit, but I find that the cornstarch sometimes makes it a little gelatinous, like canned pie filling, and I'd rather a crisp be a little runny and full of sweet, warm, bursted berry juice than too gummy. And I want a short recipe list, especially in the summer. I can manage oats. Almond meal is the outer edge. Cornstarch? Impossible.

I eat this for breakfast, sometimes with a few spoonfuls of Greek yogurt. And it's great after dinner, still warm, with melty scoops of vanilla ice cream.

Like all my favorite recipes, this one is endlessly adaptable. When I'm out of maple syrup, brown sugar does the trick—it adds a little more sweetness and a little more crunch. And if I'm out of pecans, walnuts are great too.

Ingredients

4 cups blueberries (or almost any fruit, really)

Crisp topping:

1 cup old-fashioned oats

½ cup raw, unsalted pecans, halved or chopped

½ cup almond meal (available at Trader Joe's or health food stores, or made easily by putting almonds in food processor until fine, but before they turn to almond butter)

¼ cup maple syrup

¼ cup olive oil

½ teaspoon salt

Instructions

Mix together the crisp ingredients.

Pour the berries into an 8 by 8 pan, and then layer the crisp topping over it.

Bake at 350 degrees 35 to 40 minutes, or up to 10 minutes longer if topping and fruit are frozen, until fruit is bubbling and topping is crisp and golden.

SERVES: 4 to 6

what the table is for

The light is fading, the sky bleaching from blue to white and then warming to the softest blush pink, like ballet tights, like a rosewater macaroon. I'm worn-out and the house is ragged, but my mind and heart are full from last night's little celebration for Brannon's baby, the fourth Cooking Club shower in a year.

It was a lovely, wild night—babies everywhere, dishes sprawled all over the kitchen, platters of brisket and plates of macaroons fighting for space among wineglasses and forks and ramekins that used to hold bread pudding.

Brannon insisted it wasn't a shower—she insisted on no invitations, no fuss, nothing formal or showery. But we reminded her that she's not the boss of us, and if we wanted to celebrate her baby boy, we could celebrate all we wanted. A compromise was reached: Cooking Club as usual, with a few extra friends and a special "mini" theme to celebrate the new mini-man who would join our little family in a few months.

The Cooking Club began when Aaron and I moved back to Chicago from Grand Rapids three years ago. There are six of us—my cousins Melody and Amanda, who are sisters and both teachers; our friend Casey, whom Melody and I have known since junior high; Brannon, my stylish and sophisticated college roommate and dear friend; and Margaret, an actor and screenwriter and friend from church. Our friend from South Haven, Josilyn, was an original member until she moved away.

We meet once a month, and sometimes more, and whoever's hosting picks the theme and cooks the main course, and then the rest of us fill in around that—appetizers, sides, desserts. Or at least that's how we started. It's a little looser now. Amanda tends to remind us of the themes we keep saying we want to do. Melody and Casey cook main courses. I tend toward appetizers and side dishes. Amanda almost always does a salad and a dessert, often an ice cream. Margaret is also a baker, and Brannon always brings cocktails.

True to form, on that night, Melody brought mini-brisket sandwiches on soft white buns, and Margaret made tiny ramekins of chocolate chip bread pudding. I made mini mac & cheeses and cups of tomato soup with little grilled cheese sandwiches balancing on top. Casey poured her famous green goddess dressing into the bottoms of juice glasses, then filled the glasses with raw veggies—slim carrots and celery and cucumber. Our friend Emily came in from Michigan with mini loaves of her grandmother's poppy seed cake, which I requested because I love it, especially with coffee, for breakfast.

There's always a little chaos right when everyone arrives—bringing in hot dishes, shrugging off coats, lifting babies out of car seats. We bump the oven temp up and down; we go into one another's drawers for knives and cutting boards and platters. We chop herbs, assemble sandwiches, dress and toss salads. The once-empty spaces of our homes become overrun with baskets, coats, shoes, things we've borrowed and are now returning, cake plates, baby clothes, cookbooks. We swirl around each other, hugging hello, opening wine, lifting down glasses from the highest shelves.

Mel and Amanda are always early. Margaret is always late. Mel, Brannon, and I all collect red Le Creuset pans and bakeware, so it can get a little confusing, but Casey has orange everything, so you can always tell what's hers. Brannon is always arriving with what seems like a truckload of furniture and bags—things she's bringing for us to borrow, things she picked up at the store that reminded her of one of us, bassinets and baby slings and bottles.

That afternoon, as I got the house ready for Brannon's "don't-call-it-a-shower" shower, I thought that even though the Cooking Club always, always sits around the table, this time it might be nice to sit in the living room. I moved furniture, made a place for presents, and set up a buffet on the round table in the living room.

When everyone was assembled, when there was a fork or serving spoon on each platter and everything was sliced and warm and ready, I tried to move everyone to the living room, and it just didn't work. I kept urging them toward the buffet, toward the couches and chairs in the living room. Finally, though, I admitted defeat, and we pulled a love seat up to the dining room table for extra seating and settled in happily. That's where we belong, it seems—around the table.

When Josilyn moved to Haiti, she wrote us a letter to say good-bye. And in that letter she wrote this line: *I can't imagine life without a table between us.* Yes. Yes. Exactly that. I can't imagine life without a table between us. The table is the life raft, the center point, the home base of who we are together.

It's those five faces around the table that keep me sane, that keep me safe, that protect me from the pressures and arrows and land mines of daily life. And it isn't because we do all the same things, live all the same ways, believe all the same things. We are single and married, liberal and conservative, runners and adamant nonathletes, mothers and not. Those of us who are mothers do it differently, from cry-it-out to family bed, from stay-at-home to full-time work. Around this table we've mourned the loss of eight pregnancies, and even as I write those words, it seems a cruel and unusual number.

We've gone to funerals and birthday parties together, reported bad test results, gotten advice about sick kids, made trips to the ER, walked together through postpartum depression. We've visited each other's babies in the hospital, and we've brought over meals and sleepers and blankets. We've talked about faith and fear and fighting with our husbands, sleeping through the night and anxiety and how to ask for help when we need it.

On the hardest days, when Brannon's daughter Emme had surgery, or when Casey's stepdad passed away, when something breaks apart or scares us, we send around a quick group email, even as our hands are shaking, even while the pain is slicing. We fill everyone in, ask for prayer, let everyone know how they can help with meals or with the kids, and at the end of the email, someone always says, *Thanks for being my people*. Or, *Glad you're my people*. Or, *What would I do without my people?*

That's what this is about. This isn't about recipes. This is about a family, a tribe, a little band of people who walk through it all together, up close and in the mess, real time and unvarnished.

And it all started around the table, once a month and sometimes more. We bump into one another in the kitchen, sliding pans in and out of the oven, setting and resetting the timer. We know one another's kitchens by heart—where Casey keeps her knives and how many pans will fit in Brannon's oven. It seems like we've been meeting together forever, but we realized last night that it's been three years this month, and that's worth remembering for me—that it doesn't take a decade, and it doesn't take three times a week.

Once a month, give or take, for three years, and what we've built is impressive—strong, complex, multifaceted. Like a curry or boeuf bourguignon, something you cook for hours and hours, allowing the flavors to develop over time, changing and deepening with each passing hour on the heat.

You don't always know what's going to come of it, but you put the time in anyway, and then, after a long, long time, you realize with great clarity why you put the time in: for this night, for these hours around the table, for the complexity and richness of flavors that are so lovely and unexpected you're still thinking about them the next day.

That's how I am today, still kind of mesmerized by last night, by the taste of Amanda's butterscotch budino and the little pile of baby clothes for the boy who will be born later this month, by the laughter and the baby noises, by the faces of my people, feeling like this is what life is for, this is what Sunday nights are for, this is what the table is for.

Mini Mac & Cheese

This is a mash-up of Grace Parisi's three-cheese mini macs from Food & Wine *and another* Food & Wine *macaroni & cheese called, appropriately enough, Macaroni and Cheese.*[1]

Be generous when you dust the Parmesan, both in the empty cups and on top, because that's what holds them together—that and the egg yolk.

These can be made gluten-free, obviously, by using brown rice or corn pasta, which is usually what I do. Watch the cook time on the pasta, as gluten-free pastas seem to be a little more unpredictable than conventional pastas.

Ingredients

½ pound elbow macaroni (or 4 cups cooked)
2 cups sharp cheddar cheese, shredded

2 tablespoons butter, plus more for pan
1 tablespoon Dijon
2 dashes Tabasco
½ teaspoon salt
1 egg yolk
½ cup grated Parmesan cheese
Smoked paprika

Instructions

In a pot of boiling water, cook the macaroni for about 5 minutes, to just al dente, which is just a touch firmer than how you'd like to eat it. Drain.

Brush mini muffin pan with melted butter, then sprinkle half the grated Parmesan into the muffin cups.

On medium-low heat, warm butter and cheddar cheese, and whisk till smooth.

Off heat, add Dijon, Tabasco, egg yolk, and whisk again.

Add macaroni and mix until well coated with cheese.

Spoon into muffin cups, making them slightly rounded and packing them lightly. Top with grated Parmesan.

Bake at 425 for 12 to 14 minutes, until golden on top.

Let cool at least 10 minutes before serving, because they will set as they cool. Sprinkle with smoked paprika.

Serve warm or at room temperature.

MAKES: 24 mini macs—the perfect amount for an appetizer at a dinner party for 8. For a cocktail party, double the recipe, using a whole box (1 pound) of pasta.

---

1. "Three-Cheese Mini Macs" recipe, first published in *Food & Wine* magazine, December 2007; "Macaroni and Cheese" recipe; first published in "Quick from Scratch Pasta," 1996.

hungry

Years ago, when I worked at a church in Grand Rapids, I drove in early on Sunday mornings, when 28th Street was still silent and gray, as the pale morning sun rose over the pawn shops and used-car dealerships. I worked all morning, talking with people, holding a thousand tiny details in my mind, and when I left in the afternoon, head spinning and feet tired, I always hoped I was in the car in time to hear *The Splendid Table* on NPR. It was a good day if I made it to the car in time for it, and a bad day if I missed it and turned on the radio only to hear *A Prairie Home Companion* instead, because it meant I'd stayed longer than I'd intended and because, to be honest, I really don't like *A Prairie Home Companion*.

Lynne Rossetto Kasper, the host of *The Splendid Table*, says there are two kinds of people in the world: people who wake up thinking about what to have for supper and people who don't. I am in the first camp, certainly. But it took me about twenty years to say that out loud.

I've always been hungry. Always. I remember being hungry as a small child, as an adolescent girl, as an adult, and just after I locate those feelings and memories of hunger, in my peripheral vision another thing buzzes up, like a flash of heat or pain: shame. Hunger, then shame. Hunger, then shame. Always hungry, always ashamed.

I have always been on the round side of average, sometimes the very round side and sometimes just a little round. I was a round-faced, chubby baby, a little girl with soft, puffy cheeks, a teenager who longed to be skinny and never was, who routinely threw all her pants on the floor and glared at them like enemies. A woman who still longs to be skinny and never is, and who still, from time to time, throws all her pants on the floor and glares at them like enemies. After all these years, the heaviest thing isn't the number on the scale but the weight of the shame I've carried all these years—*too big, too big, too big.*

I've always wanted to be thinner, and I've always loved to eat, and I felt betrayed by my appetites. Why couldn't I be one of those people who forgets to eat? Or who can't eat a bite when she's stressed or sad? When I'm stressed or sad, I eat like a truffle pig, hoping that great mouthfuls of food will make me feel tethered to something, grounded, safe. And I eat when I'm happy too—when the table is full of people I love, when we're celebrating.

My appetite is strong, powerful, precise, but for years and years, I tried to pretend I couldn't hear it screaming in my ears. It wasn't ladylike. It wasn't proper. So I pretended I wasn't hungry, pretended I'd already eaten, murmured something about not caring one way or the other, because I was afraid that my appetites would get the best of me, that they would expose my wild and powerful hunger.

I learned something about hunger from my friend Sara. Sara was one of the first women I knew who ate like a man. When she was hungry, she announced it. And then she ate. A lot. We were traveling through Europe together in college, when I was in the throes of a deep and desperate hatred toward my body. I watched Sara with confusion and fascination, the way a child watches an animal he's never seen—wide-eyed and kind of nervous. If Sara was hungry while we were on our way to a play, she'd ask us to stop. Because she was hungry. All of us stopped because she was hungry. I would have sooner lost consciousness on the sidewalk than draw attention to my hunger and, therefore, my body.

I realized that even most of the thin women I knew had learned to demur about food and hunger—*I already ate; I couldn't possibly; I'm absolutely stuffed.* But Sara loved to eat and believed it was her right, and a pleasure. She didn't overeat or undereat, cry or hide food. She just ate, for sustenance and enjoyment both, and I was fascinated. Still, it took almost a decade more for me to say those words—*those words, "I'm hungry"*—without feeling ashamed.

It took becoming pregnant to finally say to the world, out loud and without embarrassment, *I'm hungry.* My first pregnancy shifted so many aspects of my understanding of my body and, with it, shifted my view of hunger. Even if at twenty-nine years old I couldn't claim my own hunger without experiencing a shiver of shame, I could claim hunger on behalf of my baby, and that small step might as well have been a mile for all it unlocked inside me.

Several years later, I'm learning to practice gratitude for a healthy body, even if it's rounder than I'd like it to be. I'm learning to take up all the space I need, literally and figuratively, even though we live in a world that wants women to be tiny and quiet. To feed one's body, to admit one's hunger, to look one's appetite straight in the eye without fear or shame—this is controversial work in our culture.

Part of being a Christian means practicing grace in all sorts of big and small and daily ways, and my body gives me the opportunity to demonstrate grace, to make peace with imperfection every time I see myself in the mirror. On my best days, I practice grace and patience with myself, knowing that I can't extend grace and patience if I haven't tasted it.

I used to think the goal was to get over things—to deal with them once and for all, to snap an issue closed like slamming a locker door, washing my hands of it forever and always. What I know now after all these years is that there are some things you don't get over, some things you just make friends with at a certain point, because they've been following you around like a stray dog for years.

That's how this is for me. I've been catastrophizing about my weight since I was six. I've lost the pounds and gained them, made and abandoned plans and promises, cried tears of frustration, pinched the backs of my upper arms with a hatred that scares me.

And through all that, I've made friends and fallen in love, gotten married and become a mother. I've written and traveled and stayed up late with people I love. I've walked on the beach and on glittering city streets. I've kissed my baby's cheeks and danced with my husband and laughed till I cried with my best friends, and through all that it didn't really matter that I was heavier than I wanted to be.

The extra pounds didn't matter, as I look back, but the shame that came with those extra pounds was like an infectious disease. That's what I remember. And so these days, my mind and my heart are focused less on the pounds and more on what it means to live without shame, to exchange that heavy and corrosive self-loathing for courage and freedom and gratitude. Some days I do just that, and some days I don't, and that seems to be just exactly how life is.

Back to Lynne Rossetto Kasper. I wake up in the morning and I think about dinner. I think about the food and the people and the things we might discover about life and about each other. I think about the sizzle of oil in a pan and the smell of rosemary released with a knife cut. And it could be that that's how God made me the moment I was born, and it could be that that's how God made me along the way as I've given up years of secrecy and denial and embarrassment. It doesn't matter at this point. What matters is that one of the ways we grow up is by declaring what we love.

I love the table. I love food and what it means and what it does and how it feels in my hands. And that might be healthy, and it might be a reaction to a world that would love me more if I starved myself, and it's probably always going to be a mix of the two. In any case, it's morning and I'm hungry. Which is not the same as weak or addicted or shameful. I'm hungry. And I'm thinking about dinner, not just tonight, but the next night and the next. There are two kinds of people, and I'm tired of pretending I'm the other.

Nigella's Flourless Chocolate Brownies
Adapted from Nigella Express

I have a serious thing for Nigella Lawson's cookbooks. I read them like novels, and at the end of especially long days, I read them in bed before I go to sleep—comfort food for my brain. She writes about food in a way that connects with me, that captures appetite and passion and celebration and flavor in a way that moves me. Back when I couldn't admit my own hunger, Nigella's books became very dear to me because she did just that in a way that I wasn't yet able to do. She's not at all daunted or afraid of her appetites, and she has been a guide for me along that path.

I'm not always wild about flourless chocolate cake, and it's not for lack of trying. Because Aaron eats gluten-free, we've tested lots of flourless chocolate cakes and tarts and brownies, and often they seem kind of egg-heavy to me, kind of like a not-so-good custard. But the almond meal in these brownies makes them heavy and dense in such a good way, and the addition of almond extract makes them even more fragrant and rich. I cut them into quite small pieces, almost like fudge. Heavenly.

And I've found that almost any good chocolate works for these— semisweet chips, a dark chocolate bar cut into chunks, anything. You really can't go wrong.

Ingredients

- 1 cup semisweet chocolate chips
- 1 cup butter
- 1 cup sugar
- 1 teaspoon vanilla
- 1 teaspoon almond extract
- 3 eggs, beaten
- 1½ cups almond meal or ground almonds
- 1 cup walnuts, chopped

Instructions

Preheat the oven to 325 degrees. Melt the chocolate and butter over low heat in a saucepan, stirring until glossy and smooth.

Take the pan off heat, mix in the vanilla, sugar, and almond extract, and let it cool for just a few minutes.

Stir the eggs into the saucepan, then add the ground almonds and chopped walnuts and stir again. The batter will be a little grainy at this point because of the almonds, but don't worry a bit.

Pour batter into an 8 by 8 pan, and bake for 25 to 30 minutes, until the top has set but the brownies are still a little wiggly. Let cool completely, then cut into 16 small squares.

start where you are

My friend Laura's New Year's resolution is "start where you are." I love it, and I think it can be applied to almost everything. Whatever thing seems too intimidating or enormous, whatever new skill seems too far off to develop, whatever project has been hanging over your head for what seems like forever: *start where you are.*

I believe every person should be able to make the simple foods that nourish them, that feel familiar and comforting, that tell the story of who they are. Each one of us should be able to nourish ourselves in the most basic way and to create meals and traditions around the table that tell the story of who we are to the people we care about. And the only way to get there is to start where you are.

If you don't cook, begin by inviting people over. Order pizza and serve it with a green salad and a bottled salad dressing. Get comfortable with people in your home, with the mess and the chaos. Focus on making people comfortable, on creating a space protected from the rush and chaos of daily life, a space full of laughter and safety and soul.

Then next time or the time after that, try grilled flatbread pizzas, and make your own vinaigrette for the salad. The next time, try a dessert and an appetizer, and little by little, build a sense of muscle memory, a body of knowledge, a set of patterns for how your home and your heart open and expand when the people you love are gathered around your table.

We've been told that cooking and baking and entertaining are specialized skills that only some people possess, and that without a culinary degree or a lifestyle brand we can't be expected to do anything but buy prepared food. Marketing and advertising campaigns urging us to eat out or buy already prepared foods want us to think that plain old cooking is difficult and not worth learning. This trend began in the 1950s after factories that used to make ammunition had to make something else. So they started making shelf-stable food in cans and boxes, similar to what soldiers had been eating but unfamiliar to the average American family. In order to sell canned food and cake mixes, advertisers had to convince American women that cooking is too hard and troublesome for our modern world. But it wasn't true then, and it isn't true now.

It takes some time to learn, to try and fail and make a mess and try again. It takes even longer to get truly comfortable, to feel at home with a knife in your hand, to read through recipes as a guideline or set of ideas, to read through and add your preferences and tastes, your history and perspective. But it's a lovely process, with not a minute wasted. If you put in the time, the learning, the trying, the mess, and the failure, at the end you will have learned to feed yourself and the people you love, and that's a skill for life—like tennis or piano but yummier and far less expensive.

I'm not talking about cooking as performance, or entertaining as a complicated choreography of competition and showing off. I'm talking about feeding someone with honesty and intimacy and love, about making your home a place where people are fiercely protected, even if just for a few hours, from the crush and cruelty of the day.

I always wanted a home filled with people. Our home growing up was quite private. My dad worked long hours at our church, and my mom is an introvert, and those two dynamics created a home that was quiet, private, safe. It was exactly right for my family, but at the same time, I longed for a little loud. I wanted a full table, glasses clinking, laughter bubbling up over the music. I wanted cars parked all the way down the street, and people who came in without knocking, so familiar with our home that they mixed their own drinks and knew where to put the dishes after drying them.

When I moved into my own house, that's exactly what I did. The day I closed on it, I invited a bunch of friends over. It was completely empty because I hadn't yet moved in any furniture, so we sat in a circle on plastic deck chairs, eating chips and salsa served on one of those little tables you roll up and take to the beach or to outdoor concerts. I filled that little town house with people I loved every chance I got—welcome-to-town parties and going-away parties, gatherings for award shows and dinner parties.

I didn't cook almost at all because I didn't really know how. I made pasta with jarred sauce and big salads with bottled dressing, and when California Pizza Kitchen started selling their frozen pizzas at our grocery store, I think I served their Thai chicken pizza with gin and tonics and coconut hot fudge sundaes to everyone who came over that year.

Over time, though, I found myself more and more curious about what I was eating and what I was serving. When you're dependent on prepared foods, you don't get to decide how something is seasoned. You don't get to use basil in the summer and fennel in the winter. You don't get to add flavor according to your geography, your story, your table.

And I wanted to know how things worked. How does onion change the taste of a soup? Why do curry and apples and squash go together so well? Why are there so many recipes that pair bacon and brussels sprouts? I started buying cookbooks and reading them cover to cover in bed before turning out the lights at the end of the day. I wasn't cooking yet, but I was learning about flavors, about what does and doesn't go with what. I was learning about techniques for different cuts of meat and seasonal availability and regional food traditions. I was still serving frozen pizza to guests around my table, but every night I learned a little bit more. I began to understand some of the nuances between, say, Ina Garten's luxurious, classic American tastes and Art Smith's sophisticated Southern sensibilities and Nigella Lawson's lovely English way of thinking about food. I learned that Belgian-style mussels are steamed in beer, while French-style are steamed in white wine, and even though it would be more than a decade till I steamed mussels myself, I started cooking the way I start everything: by reading.

Reading is a great place to begin, but there is no substitute for hands, knife, pan. When I finally did cook mussels all those years later—French-style, of course—I knew to scrub and rinse them, to debeard them, and to discard ones that were already open before cooking and ones that didn't open over heat. I knew to serve them with hunks of crusty bread to sop up the juices. What I didn't know is that debearding is harder than it sounds, and that the grit on the shells takes so many rinses to wash away. I didn't know that the smell would be somewhere between heaven and the ocean itself —all those shallots, all that wine. I didn't know that they'd steam so fast and that before I knew it, I'd be serving this great steaming pot of amazing smells, and I couldn't have predicted that I'd feel so impossibly proud, standing before this pot.

It was like making magic, like pulling a rabbit from a hat. The words on the page don't do it justice. They never do. At a certain point, you have to pick up a knife. You have to start where you are.

The first summer we were married, Aaron declared it to be the summer of golf, which meant I had lots of long Saturdays free to putter around the kitchen for hours at a time. We still ate frozen pizza or Kraft Mac & Cheese for dinner many nights, but sometimes on those Saturdays, I'd fumble my way through marinara or key lime pie. People had given us a great assortment of cookbooks as wedding presents, and I lined them up on the windowsill above the sink in our little kitchen. We left the window open one night and a rainstorm soaked them, so their pages are a little crackly and warped, but that summer I cooked through several of them, crackly and warped though they were.

I started, as everyone should, I think, with Mark Bittman's *How to Cook Everything*. But because I am a truly terrible recipe follower, there were some bumps. I made a fresh marinara to serve over pasta one Friday night, and I misjudged how long tomatoes need to cook to lose their acidity, and much more important, I grossly underestimated how long garlic needs to mellow. I served Aaron and myself heaping portions of essentially raw tomatoes and garlic. Our tongues burned for hours. We offended people ten feet away at a football game later that night, and days after, raw garlic was still rising out of our pores. It was like drinking lighter fluid with a dash of Tabasco.

Around that same time, on the topic of lighter fluid, I attempted key lime pie. It was a recipe of shortcuts—sweetened condensed milk, frozen limeade—and it suggested at the end that if I added just a touch of tequila and then a little salt to the crust, we'd have a margarita pie on our hands. That's much more exciting than key lime, of course, so I added one large glug of tequila, but after stirring, I found I could hardly taste it. I added a few more, and a few more—I really wanted just a bit of that good tequila bite. I didn't realize that what I ended up making was a pie so full of alcohol that I should have taken people's keys before serving one slice.

Some of my gravest errors have been logistic, if not expressly culinary. One October, I was looking for a non-turkey main course to bring to a fall-themed dinner at a friend's house. I'm not a huge turkey fan, and I remembered that a few years ago, the Thanksgiving cover of *Gourmet* magazine featured a pumpkin filled with soup as the centerpiece of the Thanksgiving table instead of the turkey. I found a recipe that was almost like a french onion soup—layers of homemade croutons, shredded Gruyère, lots of fresh sage, all soaked in broth and cooked for hours in a large pumpkin.

Everything was going swimmingly until I realized I was going to have to transport a fifteen-pound pumpkin filled to the top with simmering hot liquid.

It took a cardboard box, a laundry basket, several wire cooling racks, a roll of heavy-duty aluminum foil, and every beach towel in the house, but I did finally make it to Casey's house with the pumpkin intact, after driving twenty miles an hour and rolling through every stop.

That's the fun, that's the adventure of it. There's always something to try, something completely new that builds on old techniques, a new set of flavors for an old classic, a skill from one recipe that is just the thing for another. And then sometimes you end up cradling a burning-hot fifteen-pound soup-filled pumpkin like a baby, and you could never have seen that one coming.

One of the best feelings, I think, is when you learn to make something you didn't even know regular people can make. I remember the first time I saw someone make salad dressing. My friend Tecia from summer camp was living in Lyon, France, the year after we graduated from college. I visited her for a few weeks, and one day as she made lunch, I watched her very casually smash a garlic clove, spoon in some Dijon, add some vinegar, and then whisk the whole thing with one hand while streaming in olive oil with the other. This was before I'd started cooking with any real regularity, and salad dressing was something I'd never thought about making myself.

It took a few years to try it myself, but now I always have a jar or two of vinaigrette on my counter, and it always makes me think of Tecia in that dim French kitchen when I whisk Dijon and vinegar together before streaming in the oil.

Some people—like my friend Sara who currently lives in Botswana—prefer a little sweetness in a vinaigrette, either a pinch of sugar or a dab of honey or maple syrup. But I like a very vinegary vinaigrette. The beauty of vinaigrette is that you can make it a thousand ways, according to what you have on hand, according to the greens you're dressing or your particular tastes.

So save a pickle jar or a jelly jar, and every few days, make yourself a vinaigrette. You'll feel like you're practicing magic, or like you've turned water into wine.

Basic Vinaigrette

A vinaigrette is usually 3 parts oil to 1 part acid, but I tend to do 2 parts oil to 1 part acid because I love that sharp, puckery vinegar taste. The vinaigrette I make most often is so simple—just Dijon, balsamic vinegar, salt, pepper, and olive oil.

First, I put a heaping spoonful of Dijon in the bottom of a jelly jar and then some big glugs of balsamic vinegar. I add a good pinch of salt and pepper and then shake it all up. Once that's all incorporated, I add olive oil, twice as much oil as there is vinegar and Dijon. Shake again and then taste. If it's entirely too puckery for you, start your adjustment by adding half a teaspoon of sugar and see how that tastes.

Making vinaigrette is all about making it your own, tasting as you go, adjusting bit by bit, and the best way to taste it is to dip a lettuce leaf in the vinaigrette and see how it tastes on the leaf. Greens vary so much from mild butter lettuce to peppery arugula, so it's a good idea to get into the habit of making your vinaigrette according to the flavor of the greens you're dressing. Arugula will need more sweetness, and a mild butter lettuce can't stand up to a very puckery-sharp bite of vinegar.

Some people like to make vinaigrette in a bowl, mixing the acids first and then whisking in the oil in a stream. Some people recommend using the food processor so that everything blends together vigorously and gets all finely chopped along the way. I like the jelly jar—the shaking of it, the simplicity of it. I like having a jar on my counter next to my stove, always at the ready, to pour over greens or rice or soup.

Traditional french vinaigrette begins with a minced shallot, Dijon, red wine vinegar, and olive oil. If you like a creamier dressing, add a bit of goat cheese or crumbled feta, and you can always add fresh and dried herbs too, according to your taste. Lemon and a minced garlic clove make a bright, flavorful dressing, and oregano and thyme slant it toward the Mediterranean, perfect for Greek salads.

People use lots of different oils, but flavored oils aren't my thing. I use extra virgin olive oil for just about everything. Sometimes I use white balsamic or red wine vinegar or apple cider vinegar, but my favorite is balsamic—I put it on just about everything. And instead of vinegar, you can use a citrus juice as your acid—pink grapefruit juice is lovely in a vinaigrette over baby spinach, and I use lime juice with white balsamic in a dressing that goes over watermelon feta salad.

Ingredients

- 1 tablespoon Dijon
- ¼ cup balsamic vinegar
- ¼ teaspoon salt
- ⅛ teaspoon pepper
- ½ cup olive oil

Instructions

Spoon Dijon into an old jelly jar, then add vinegar and salt and pepper. Screw on the lid tightly and shake vigorously. Then add the oil, replace the lid, and shake again. Dip your finger in to taste, and

go-to risotto

Risotto is my go-to entertaining meal. I like the process of it
—toasting the arborio rice, the brash sizzle when the wine hits
the pan. Risotto lets you know what's happening at every turn.
Risotto-making is the exact opposite of baking, where it all
happens in the oven without you. Risotto shouts out each step,
invites you to notice each change. It's physical and active and clear.
I like that about risotto. It's also endlessly versatile. Shrimp and
peas? Asparagus and lemon zest? Sundried tomatoes?—so many
options.

The first time I made risotto, it was a recipe for coconut black
bean risotto, and I was unaware, apparently, that risotto is a
traditionally Italian dish, and that coconut and black beans both
were quite a stretch. But then maybe that was a good thing,
because it taught me right away how incredibly elastic this
meal is.

Risotto is the absolute perfect mix of fancy and comforting
at the same time, and all my favorite foods fall into that category
—goat cheese scrambled eggs, mango chicken curry, bacon-
wrapped dates. And it's naturally gluten-free, and is easily made
dairy-free, vegetarian, or even vegan. Try thinking of something
that's gluten-free, vegan, and more sustaining than a plate of
greens: risotto made with vegetable stock—hurrah!

There's a lot of fuss about how hard risotto is, about how you have to stand at the stove and stir tirelessly for an hour. Yes, and no. You don't have to stir every second. But you don't want to leave the room either. You want to make this when the kitchen is full anyway, when there's a platter of bread and cheese within your reach, when you've already opened the wine. The stirring's not so bad, but it does always take longer than I think it will, so allow yourself lots of time, and make sure your guests have plenty of cheese and wine in the meantime.

In his beautiful cookbook *A Platter of Figs*, David Tanis says that when you're making risotto, the cooking level you're looking for will yield "sinkholes"—not a wild boil, not an entirely uneventful simmer, but little round depressions that pop a little. Sinkholes, exactly.

If the rest of the meal is flavorful and show-offy, I'll keep the risotto as simple as possible. I think the perfect New Year's Eve dinner would be tiny little steaks or perfectly plain steamed lobster with champagne and Parmesan risotto. A lightly dressed bowl of greens, maybe, with a shallot and lemon vinaigrette, and ice-cold champagne. Dreamy.

I love risotto with shrimp and bacon, and to get an even richer bacon flavor, I cook the beginning onions and garlic in bacon fat. I do the same thing with mushrooms when I'm making a mushroom and bacon risotto, or I cook the mushrooms in cognac in a separate little pan and add them about five minutes from the end.

You can use whatever wine you like, knowing that the risotto will carry some of the flavor. Pinot grigio is a natural choice, but I do like a buttery, oaky Chardonnay. Champagne or sparkling white wine is lovely in it, and you can also use red wine if you'd like, and the whole thing will be slightly pink. When I do that, I add lots of fresh spinach too so that it doesn't look like a Valentine's dish gone terribly wrong.

I add peas and asparagus and basil in the spring, or roasted butternut squash in the fall. The key, I've found, to butternut squash risotto is to roast the squash, whole and unpeeled, the day before, and then when it cools, peel and scoop out the flesh. Add it right near the end of cooking, all mushy and orange and delicious. I add nutmeg and sage to that one, but I suppose you could add a little curry, and even a diced apple for sweetness.

I know, I know. There are some people who would say because it's an Italian dish, it must be treated with an Italian sensibility. I get that. I'm not a huge fan of kooky fusion stuff, like tacos with wasabi and ginger or ravioli filled with barbecue.

But our goal, remember, is to feed around our table the people we love. We're not chefs or restaurateurs or culinary school graduates, and we shouldn't try to be. Make it the way the people you love want to eat it. Make it the way you love it. Try it a million ways and cross a few off the list because they were terrible, but celebrate the fact that you found a few new ways too—ways that are fresh and possibly unconventional but perfect for your family. That's the goal.

Learn, little by little, meal by meal, to feed yourself and the people you love, because food is one of the ways we love each other, and the table is one of the most sacred places we gather. If you feel paralyzed in the kitchen because you don't know the rules or can't make a plan or fear making a mess, I hope you throw caution to the wind anyway and try a few new things. If you long to entertain but don't feel Martha Stewart-y enough for all that, I hope you dive in and give it a shot anyway, imperfect and nerve-racking as it may be the first few times.

And begin with risotto.

Basic Risotto

If you're a recipe stickler, this one is going to drive you crazy. Risotto is one of those dishes you just have to try a few times yourself, to teach yourself the moves and sounds and smells and textures. This is a guide map, but kind of a rough and tattered one. Try it for the first time when the stakes are low. This is not something you want to try for the first time for fussy guests or in-laws. Try this one in an empty house on a rainy night. Put on an album you love, open the wine, and give it a shot. Once you've tasted it, seen it, smelled it along the way, then you're in business, and you can make it for even your trickiest guest. I've made it for everyone I know, I think, and it's always a hit—that perfect blend of comforting and fancy all in one bowl.

Ingredients

Olive oil
4 cloves of garlic
1 onion
2 cups arborio rice
1 cup white wine
6 cups chicken broth
Parmesan cheese
Salt and pepper to taste

Instructions

Begin by putting 6 cups of chicken broth in a small pot over low heat to warm up, and then chop the onions—not a fine chop—just so they're slender and bite-able.

Let a thin layer—not too thin, but not a pool—of olive oil heat up in a dutch oven or stockpot, and then add the onions. Let them soften on medium to medium-low for five minutes or so while you press four cloves of garlic.

I've had a garlic press for years, and just learned from my friend Matt that you don't actually need to peel the cloves before smashing them through the press—so good to know. So I press four cloves of garlic and drop them in the pan with the warm oil. Then I give it maybe three more minutes, till the onions are translucent and the garlic smell fills the house.·

When the garlic and onion smell fantastic, throw in the arborio rice. The rice sizzles and pops in the oil for a while, so stir, stir, stir, and then when it seems to be coated thoroughly, add in a big glassful of wine, and stir, stir, stir. Wooden spoon, by the way.

The wine will release a fantastic smell. Give it a little time to soften, and then when the wine is absorbed, add a cup of warmed broth and again stir, stir, stir.

Basically, at this point, you're trying to keep it from drowning, and keep it from drying out. So add a little bit more broth, stir a little bit more; feel free to turn down the heat if it feels a little out of control. Not aggressive boiling, not lazy simmering. Remember the sinkholes. Keep adding broth cup by cup. Stir every few minutes.

Every recipe I've read says 18 to 20 minutes from this point, but to be honest, it always takes me longer—more like 30 to 35 minutes. Keep tasting along the way, and when you've added 6-ish cups of broth and when the rice feels soft at first but still with a bite in the middle, you're there.

I think some people may get into trouble with risotto because they expect there to be no gritty hardness at the center of each grain, so they overcook by a long shot. As long as you know there will always be that·hard little center, you won't overcook.

While you're watching, stirring, and adding stock from time to time, you can dream about what you'd like to throw in at the end.

One great option: slice up a whole bunch of mushrooms—as many kinds as you like—and soften them in a tablespoon or so of butter. When they're soft, pour in some cognac or white wine and cook just a little longer. When the risotto is cooked, stir in the mushrooms and their yummy juices from the pan.

Just two more things to throw in at this point: first, Parmesan cheese—a handful mixed in, and a small handful to throw on top right at the end. Finish with a couple rough grinds of black pepper, and there you go.

SERVES: 4 to 6

enough

Something extraordinary happened to me today. I found out a dear friend is pregnant. That's not extraordinary. Everyone I know is pregnant. You think I'm exaggerating, but I have seventeen pregnant friends, and nine friends with babies born since September. Not just Facebook friends or acquaintances either —real see-them-at-church, go-to-their-showers, send-them-baby-blankets friends.

It's an epidemic, and I sometimes think I might be at the center of it—like if you're my friend, you're 883,584 times more likely to get pregnant than if you're not. I'm like an incredibly successful fertility drug. My friend Kelly used to say that if you want to get married, you should be his roommate, because for a couple of years everyone who moved in with him promptly met someone, fell in love, moved out, and got married. That's how I am with pregnancies. Trying to conceive? Be my friend. It works for you, but it doesn't seem to be working for me.

Henry will be five this year, and since his first birthday, we've been trying to have another baby—seeing doctors, praying, longing. I've miscarried twice, and one of the pregnancies was twins. And in the meantime, approximately every woman I know between twenty and forty has announced a pregnancy.

At one point this winter I was feeling so tender and raw about it that at dinner with my family, I said, "If any of you is pregnant, I just need you to tell me now." I said this to my almost-sixty-year-old parents and my single brother. They stared at me with confusion, but at that point, nothing would have surprised me. My phone's probably pregnant. That chair over there probably just got pregnant without even trying.

Clearly, I was not handling this well. At one point I told Aaron, "Pregnant is the new skinny." What I meant is, if you know me at all, you know that one of my most cracked-up, terribly errant beliefs is that skinny people are always happy. Because I think I would be happy all day long if I was skinny. If something upset me, I would just look down at my long, skinny legs—happiness! If my heart was broken, I'd just put on a bikini—and that sadness would vanish.

I know this isn't true. I know this is crazy talk. I know miserable skinny people. But I confess that sometimes I want to shake them: *I know, I know, this or that has got you down, but find a three-way mirror and look at your butt. Don't you feel better now? I know I would.*

I found myself believing the same thing about being pregnant —that all my left-out, broken-down, fragile, ugly feelings would vanish the second I saw the all-important line on the pregnancy test. I know it's not true, but I felt it.

I became the person people don't want to tell they're pregnant. I hate that. A friend told me her happy, fantastic news, and just a second later she burst out crying, afraid for how this would make me feel. I hate that. I work really hard to arrange my face in such a way that approximates uncomplicated glee. And I *am* happy for them, of course. But sometimes just after the happiness is the desperation. Some days are easier than others.

At one point I told Aaron that if I found out I wasn't pregnant that month, I'd break something glass, just to feel it shatter in my hands. I was counting the days all the time, recounting, hoping.

And then I found out I wasn't pregnant. Again. I didn't break anything, but I posted something on my blog about how I was feeling. I should have been doing all sorts of other, more urgent work, but that morning at the coffee shop, all that sadness and frustration and confusion bled out of my fingers and onto the screen.

Later that week I had lunch with my friend Emily. She lives in Michigan and came in town to visit. To be honest, I hoped she hadn't read my post. She was one of my seventeen pregnant friends, and I wanted to talk about her baby and her pregnancy —about cravings and names and maternity clothes. I wanted it to be a sweet, happy lunch. And it was. We talked about all the lovely baby stuff, and then she gave me a card and a gift.

She told me that she had read my post, and that this was the point in friendship when sometimes two friends walk away from each other for a while, because the pain and the awkwardness and the tenderness was too great. She said she thought we could do better than that.

And then she handed me two pairs of safety goggles.

She said, "When you feel like shattering something, I'll be right there with you. We'll put on our safety goggles. I'll help you break something, and then I'll help you clean it up."

She said, "You've been celebrating with me, and I'll be here to grieve with you. We can do this together."

It took my breath away. We cried together at the restaurant, the two of us, one pregnant, one not, sitting next to the window of an Italian restaurant on a busy street, each with a pair of Home Depot safety goggles, tears running down our faces.

It was one of the most extraordinary experiences of friendship I've ever had. Because it would have been so easy for her to say, "I'm in my happy season. This is a wonderful, blessed season for me, and I don't want Angry Pants over here wrecking it." She could have concluded it was so complicated to manage her joy and my sadness that she wouldn't enter into this mess. But she did enter in.

Something broke inside me that day. Something cracked, and all the energy and fear and roiling anger drained out. I felt calm and empty. I felt sad but not devastated. I was exhausted and couldn't carry it anymore.

Enough.

It had reached fever pitch—consuming, obsessive, frantic. Unsustainable. It was like an addiction, and that moment was like getting sober—raw, silent, clear-eyed, the absolute stillness after a storm. It felt like praying.

When I was sitting with Emily celebrating her good news, I felt what I've wanted to feel all along but couldn't locate: uncomplicated and deep happiness. I felt happy for her. Very, very happy. And I feel so thankful for that feeling, for being able to be uncomplicatedly happy for the people I love.

It could all change again next month, I know. I've been around this block for years now: easier and harder, more complicated and less. I'm all serene and happy right now, but I could be back to throwing glassware next month. Today, though, I'll take what I can get.

Enough: I don't want to live like that anymore. And enough: I have enough. I have more than I need, more than I could ask for. I have a son who delights me every single day. A husband I adore. A family that walks with me well and friends who make the world feel rich. I do work I care about—no small thing.

It's not wrong to want another baby, but there's a fine line in there, and I feel I've crossed it a few times these last months, and moved over into that terrible territory where you can't be happy unless you have just that thing you want, no matter what else you have. Speaking of children, that's how they are—demanding, myopic, only able to focus on what they need in that moment. That's not how I want to live. That's not who I want to be.

I want to cultivate a deep sense of gratitude, of groundedness, of enough, even while I'm longing for something more. The longing and the gratitude, both. I'm practicing believing that God knows more than I know, that he sees what I can't, that he's weaving a future I can't even imagine from where I sit this morning.

Extraordinary, indeed.

More than enough.

the chopping block

Last winter I went to a weeklong culinary boot camp at The Chopping Block, a recreational cooking school in the city. Months earlier, I'd had a fantastic time with the Cooking Club girls at one of their evening classes called "April in Paris." They taught us to make mussels in white wine, a frisée salad with hazelnuts, steak au poivre, and truffled mashed potatoes, all of which were delicious, all of which have become staples in one or another of our homes. After the evening class, I found myself tempted by their boot camp—a full week of classes—and on impulse, I signed up.

The night before the boot camp began, I found myself nervous, like it was the first day of high school. Where would my locker be? What if no one talked to me? What if they were all master chefs, and I'm the girl they laugh at, the one who undercooks rice and overcooks chicken?

On the first morning, when one of the chefs asked me why I took the class, I told him that my enthusiasm for cooking had outpaced my technical skills. I still mess up lots of really easy stuff because I've never taken the time to really learn the techniques. One hazard for an avid reader is that it's easy to think you can do something just because you've read about it. Not true. Same with watching something on TV. As more and more of us watch more and more shows on the Food Network and the like, we actually cook less and less.

We think that because we log hours in front of Giada or Barefoot Contessa, we're actually cooking, so when it's time to cook, we eat cheese and crackers in front of the TV, exhausted from our imaginary and vicarious culinary exertions. I read cookbooks voraciously, and I could talk you through the steps of all kinds of things—how to make a béchamel sauce or how to debone a duck. But if you put an actual duck in front of me, I'd be lost. There's something about turning off the TV, or closing the book, and standing in front of your cutting board, knife in hand. There's no replacement for seeing exactly how an aioli comes together while you're breaking your arm whisking, or how a steak cooks on cast iron, smelling it, seeing the color change and the liquid pool on top.

On our first morning of the boot camp, Paul, the most formal of our chefs, began with knife skills. For hours we chopped and diced and minced, and learned the difference between a brunoise and a julienne. I'll never look at a carrot or an onion the same way again, and my apologies to the poor arctic char that I butchered very, very poorly.

For each recipe, the chef explained the ingredients and the techniques, and then each group of four began to prep and cook. Someone put the appropriate pan on the stove, while another passed out the vegetables and another circled the pan with oil as the heat rose. All this silently, the knives keeping time in our new song.

My classmates and I discovered that there is something almost meditative about chopping our mirepoix (pronounced *meer-pwah*) —the three things you need for almost every classic French recipe: onion, carrot, celery. Italian mirepoix: fennel, onion, shallots. If you're cooking Creole or Cajun food, it shifts a bit, and it's called the holy trinity: onion, celery, green pepper. They're the first step, the building block of almost everything, and through the week, we became near-automatic in our preparations.

We found butchering similarly meditative—in a silent kitchen, each of us pulling our knives deeper and deeper along a tendon within a beef tenderloin or the spine of a fish, carving and separating, lost in the work.

I was so curious about who'd take this class—who could or even wanted to spend a week in January in Chicago cooking from 9 to 5? As we sat around the long tables along the windows, tasting all the things we'd made, I learned my group's stories: a web usability consultant, a lawyer, a substitute teacher, and a teacher/boxer about to open her own local/seasonal market and café. In the other groups, a married couple, two sisters, and a bunch of other really nice people who just love to cook and love to eat.

We had no shortage of topics of conversation—Chicago restaurants we love, techniques we wanted to try, ingredients we couldn't get enough of and ingredients we hated. I was reminded once again that there are interesting, smart, kind people just absolutely everywhere, and that when you do things you care about, you find quick kinship with people who are passionate about those same things. It's how my husband connects with other musicians, how my brother finds sailors and motorcycle enthusiasts wherever he goes.

Cooking is so elemental, almost violent: knife, fire, chop, blaze. These are war words, and kitchen words too. Mario, our favorite chef, urged us to be less timid. He told us that the difference between restaurant cooking and home cooking—and often, too, the difference between great flavor and tasteless food—is two things: more heat and more seasoning. His constant refrain as he made his way around the kitchen: "More heat. More salt. More butter."

That deep, almost nutty color on your pan-fried chicken breasts: higher heat. That rich, silky sauce? More butter. The answer to absolutely everything else? Salt, salt, salt. What our chef called a pinch, we called practically a handful, and we were all jumpy at the beginning of the week, with roaring flames under each burner. But with each recipe and new dish, we learned that he was right—more heat, more butter, more salt.

And, of course, more butter and more salt are relative—the chefs still used far less fat and sodium than what's found in most processed meals, and they reminded us that high-quality ingredients like Maldon sea salt and good butter mean you use so much less while creating so much more flavor.

After butchery, we made soups, stocks, and the mother sauces —the five sauces that are the foundation of classic French cooking, according to Auguste Escoffier, whose giant book *Le Guide Culinaire*, written in 1903, still stands as the defining work on traditional French cooking.

One morning we made mayonnaise, aioli, hollandaise, and béchamel and sampled them all before lunch. We did eggs about a million ways, chicken piccata, homemade macaroni and cheese. One afternoon we learned how to butterfly a pork loin, and then our chef taught us to stuff it with a rich mix of balsamic-soaked prunes and toasted pine nuts. While it roasted, we made a sauce of shallots and balsamic to pour over it, and on the train on the way home, my little takeout box made our whole car smell like heaven by way of Italy.

We did steak au poivre—a classic French recipe for steaks coated with smashed peppercorns and cooked in butter in a cast-iron skillet. While the steaks rested, we deglazed the pans with cognac, whisking in Dijon, cream, and stock to make a sauce so rich and lovely I wanted to eat it with a spoon, no steak necessary.

On the last day of class, we were instructed to make any meal we wanted, incorporating the techniques we'd learned. The catch was that we'd be cooking without using recipes. Our little group decided on "local and seasonal" as a guiding theme, which meant winter in Chicago, which led us to venison and dried cherries. Chef Mario talked us through the plan—he recommended we use parsnips instead of carrots in our mirepoix, deglaze with port instead of the wine used in a traditional braise, and add the cherries after all the venison had been browned in batches.

While Kathi began the mirepoix, I butchered the venison shoulder, which is proof that people really can change. For many years, I only ate meat that was boneless because it freaked me out and made me feel overly carnivorous and animal-like to wrestle with wiggly, slippery bones. All of a sudden, fast-forward to me burying a ten-inch knife into a venison shoulder and, in the process, ending up with deer blood all over my shoes.

As the venison braised in chicken stock, port, and dried cherries, we roasted potatoes, celery root, and turnips, and when they had cooled, we gave them a rough mash with some butter, stock, and cream. The kitchen was buzzing, each group making their own elaborate menus—duck ragu over handmade pappardelle, a whole fish baked in a salt crust, paella, short ribs. We shared utensils and ingredients, running herbs and chunks of goat cheese and lemons from station to station, and then, finally, we were done. Our dishes reached from one end of the kitchen to the other, and each group took turns explaining what they'd made and why. We tasted everything, asked questions, complimented each group on their great meals. And then we were silent for a while, exhausted and consumed by the tastes and smells.

I could have stayed at that table all day, but I had to leave a few minutes early to catch a flight to an event I was speaking at the next morning. I wiped down my station, took off my chef's coat. I hugged my team, thanked the chefs, dragged my little rolling suitcase through the snow to take the train to the airport. When I got to the airport, I realized that my hair still smelled like the kitchen—warm, meaty, buttery—and that there was still venison blood on my shoes.

What I learned more than anything else that week is that we learn by doing. We learn with our hands and our noses. We learn by tasting the stock, feeling the hum of the knife back and forth, listening for the sounds of hot oil. We roll an omelet out of a pan wrong five times in a row, and then the sixth time, the whole group cheers because one of us made one perfect omelet.

Almost everything I know in the world, I learned from novels and memoirs and stories. I could practically draw you a city map of Milan, Rome, or Venice, even though I've never been to any of them. I've read about how to make the perfect Old Fashioned, how to tend a rose garden, how to butterfly a pork loin.

But then you find yourself standing at a bar or kneeling in the dirt or holding a very sharp chef's knife and you realize all at once that it doesn't matter what you've read or seen or think you know. You learn it, really learn it, with your hands. With your fingers and your knife, your nose and your ears, your tongue and your muscle memory, learning as you go.

We love the myth of the prodigy—that rare someone who is phenomenally talented without all that pesky training or work. But it is, certainly, a myth. My husband plays the piano every day, and he has for almost thirty years. People say that when he's onstage, he has an effortless quality, that he makes it look easy. He does. But they don't see the scales, the lessons, the years of playing the same hymns he learned as a child, or playing Beatles songs by ear, or picking out notes and chords late at night after we're all in bed.

Cooking is no different. There are rock stars—people whose skill or perspective propels them to the top of their field. But when you ask them how they got there, they always tell you a story about working in a diner or making pasta with a grandmother. They tell you about repetition, knife, heat, salt, butter.

The Chopping Block chefs were lovely and smart and answered all of our questions. But the most important thing they did was stand next to us as we logged the all-important hours—another onion to chop, another steak to grill, another herb to mince. Another vegetable to roast and then mash. Another egg to crack and beat, another sauce to strain and season. More heat, more butter, more salt.

Steak au Poivre with Cognac Pan Sauce
Adapted from The Chopping Block

I'm not a huge steak person, but if I'm going to eat one, this is it—the steak of my dreams. I love the peppercorns and the crust that the cast iron forms, and more than anything, I love this sauce. When I do make the steak, I serve it with roasted broccoli and roasted potatoes, and I put the sauce over everything. And sometimes I serve the sauce over chicken —even if you're not a red-meat eater, try the sauce. My prediction is that you will find yourself dreaming about it, and you might even prowl around your kitchen, looking for things to pour it over. Rice? Bread? Broccoli? Done, done, and done.

Ingredients

  6 steaks, 5 to 6 ounces each (filet mignon, New York strip, or rib eye)

  ¼ cup whole black peppercorns

      Sea salt

  2 tablespoons olive oil

  2 tablespoons butter

For the sauce:
- 2 shallots, sliced
- ½ cup cognac or brandy
- 2 tablespoons Dijon
- 1 cup chicken stock or broth
- 1 cup half and half

Instructions

Let steaks sit at room temperature on a towel for about 30 minutes to draw out moisture.

Crack peppercorns using a cast-iron skillet. Salt both sides of the steaks and then press in cracked peppercorns generously on both sides.

Heat the cast-iron skillet over medium-high heat. Add olive oil and one tablespoon of butter. When the butter is melted, add the steaks and cook on first side until there's a dark sear, 3 to 5 minutes. Flip the steaks, add remaining butter, and cook to desired doneness— 2 minutes for rare.

Remove steaks from the pan. Cover and let rest while you prepare the pan sauce.

Lower heat to medium, then add sliced shallots and cook until translucent, about 2 minutes.

Deglaze by adding cognac or brandy and scraping up the browned bits from the pan. Whisk in Dijon, chicken stock, and cream.

Turn to high heat and boil until reduced and thickened, about 5 minutes.

Serve steaks drizzled with sauce.

SERVES: 6

on tea and pajamas

During a three-month period after my last book came out, I traveled to twenty-two cities to speak at forty-four events. I went to Menlo Park and Santa Barbara and La Jolla; Dallas and Houston and Austin; Colorado Springs, Portland, and Atlanta. I spoke in churches and homes and colleges, first thing in the morning and late at night, sometimes five events in one day.

Near the end of that season, I became aware that my appetites were escalating from, say, preference to demand, from desire to obsession. The longer I was away from home, the less grounded I felt and the more intense my appetites became. At the beginning of that season, I was determined to feel great the whole time. For me, that means eating healthfully and frequently—like having salmon instead of cheese dip at dinner, and carrying mixed nuts and tea bags and water with me instead of grabbing a black coffee, not eating for eight hours, and then ordering a club sandwich and french fries from room service at midnight.

At the outset, I was vigilant. I took tea bags everywhere; I traveled with trail mix; I napped or rested between events. I was structured, boundaried, on it in every way. As time passed, though, I began to feel more frayed. I was tired, and tired of being away from home. Little by little, food became more and more important, and feeling nourished through food became increasingly central to me.

This is what I knew: I was tired and lonely in ways I couldn't recover from. I wasn't home enough between trips to get un-tired and un-lonely. I wasn't seeing my friends and family enough, and although I met wonderful people everywhere I went, I said good-bye to them at the airport. At a certain point, I was lonely for everyone.

One night in Minneapolis, I knew I needed that traveling season to be over. I asked the musician I was touring with how she felt about traveling and touring. She said, "Needle in the vein, *needle in the vein*. That's what it's like for me. I *love* it." She said she loved winning over a new audience, being charming for an evening. She said she didn't like being home for long, that she was sometimes nervous and bored between trips.

I felt just the opposite. I missed my friends and my family. I wanted to live a real, settled life, attending my friends' kids' birthday parties and not wearing a microphone so often. I was worn-out from trying to win over audiences—joke, joke, story. One more joke for the tougher crowds. I loved interacting with readers, but I was so tired and my laugh felt shrill to my own ears, and I could see by the way I was eating that my need to be fed was growing quickly into a way to nourish and love parts of myself that were frayed and starving.

On a trip to Nashville, the stress cracks were showing more than usual. It was a great trip, actually, full of familiar faces and fun events. My mother-in-law and my son were with me, so it was never lonely. But it was late in the season, and the damage had already been done. Even though the events were lovely—especially one of them that took place a little ways out of town, in the rolling hills, under a ceiling of twinkly lights, I was still too tired and scraped away to nourish myself with anything but food.

I got back late after the last event, and my mother-in-law and my son were sleeping. I sat on the carpet outside our hotel room and ate a club sandwich and french fries and drank a glass of Chardonnay. And I knew in some wordless way that I needed that sandwich more than a person should need a sandwich. I wanted, in the most obvious way, rest and care and nourishment, a sense of comfort and peace. And all I knew to do was hold on to that sandwich like it was going to run away from me. I sat there in my pajamas, covered with crumbs, and I knew I had to find a new way to live, and a new way to nourish myself along the way.

The question I couldn't answer was what it looked like to take care of myself during that season. As ever, I recreated better than I rested—when I was home between trips, I cooked, threw parties, called/texted/emailed, read, went out for dinner, shopped. But I didn't really stop, listen, feel. When I did, it scared me a little. There had to be a better way. It had to be all right to admit that I was tired, that it was hard.

I felt like my rough edges were showing all the time. I didn't like how my anger was flaring out like an automatic weapon at the smallest inconveniences. I didn't want to be run by my appetites. I felt like I was stuffing myself with food, wine, people, books, experiences, things to do. I was unbelievably productive, like a crazy Energizer Bunny, but even when I was tired, I was still consuming—wine, shows, magazines, books.

I was all feasting and no fasting—all noise, connection, go; without rest, space, silence. I was all flash and text and motion, but inside I was so tired. I was so tired I could only hear really loud music and taste really strong flavors—more, more, more. Intensity, intensity, intensity. At one event, I licked the icing off a cupcake right as I walked onstage to speak, mouth full of sugar and butter as I walked up the steps to the podium. I lost my manners and lost my ability to slow down.

What I'm finding is that when I'm hungry, lots of times what I really want more than food is an external voice to say, "You've done enough. It's OK to be tired. You can take a break. I'll take care of you. I see how hard you're trying." There is, though, no voice that can say that except the voice of God. The work I'm doing now is to let those words fall deeply on me, to give myself permission to be tired, to be weak, to need.

When I started realizing how tired I was, on the rare days that I wasn't traveling, what I wanted in the deepest way was comfort. Familiarity, warmth, memories. The best thing I could think of was a lazy morning with Henry. I'd stay in pajamas well into the afternoon, and for breakfast, I always made the same thing, a way of providing rhythm and stability.

I boiled water for tea, always Irish Breakfast, and then I softened an onion in olive oil. I added to it sliced chicken apple sausages, and in a small pot, I boiled water and then added a handful of quinoa to plump and soften. I layered the quinoa with the sausages and onions, and then topped it all with an egg, sometimes fried, still very runny in the center, and sometimes scrambled loosely with a few crumbles of goat cheese. Warm, substantial, familiar.

We all have those stretches—busy parenting seasons where the nights feel like a blink and the days wear on and on, or work deadlines that throw off our routines, or extended family commitments that pull us in a thousand directions. What heals me on those days when it all feels chaotic and swirling is the simplicity of home, morning prayer, tea, and breakfast quinoa.

Even now when I drink black tea or when I smell quinoa simmering, nutty and dense, wholesome even in its aroma, I think of those sweet mornings, of snuggling and storytelling, and strong black tea. And still now, if a morning threatens to knock me off center, I forgo the usual peanut butter toast and coffee, and I begin to boil water for tea and quinoa.

Breakfast Quinoa

This isn't really a recipe, more a glimpse into our kitchen. I've written it here to serve 4, although I mostly make it just for myself, and it's wonderful to make it all one lazy morning and then have it almost ready to go for the next three mornings. And I've written it both for a fried egg on top and a scrambled one—whatever you prefer.

Also, check the packaging on your quinoa—the kind we buy is prerinsed, but if yours isn't, you do need to give it a rinse or it will taste bitter.

Ingredients

1   tablespoon olive oil
1   large or 2 small onions
4   links chicken apple sausage (my favorites are from Trader Joe's)
2   cups quinoa
4   cups water
4   eggs
    Salt and pepper to taste

Instructions

Slice and soften onion in olive oil in a pan over medium-low heat. While that's cooking, slice the sausage and add it to the same pan.

Pour quinoa and water into a small pot. Bring it to a boil, and then turn the heat down to a simmer for about 15 minutes. Fluff with a fork, and let cool for 5 minutes.

Scoop quinoa into 4 bowls and then stir a scoop of onions and sausage slices into each one.

In the onion pan, fry the eggs to over easy, about 2 minutes over medium heat, and then slide one egg on top of the quinoa mixture in each bowl.

If you'd rather scramble the eggs, beat them and then pour them into the onion pan and begin to cook them over low heat, running a wooden spoon through them as they thicken. Scoop the loosely scrambled eggs into each bowl and top with a small handful of goat cheese. Add a sprinkle of salt and fresh ground pepper.

Note: if you're making breakfast for one, do everything the same, except only cook one egg. Cover and refrigerate the other 3 bowls, and then you've got breakfast waiting for you for the next 3 days— all you have to do is warm a bowl in the microwave and fry an egg.

SERVES: 4

run

I have long considered that there are two kinds of people in the world: people who can run marathons and people who can't. And I have long considered myself a permanent member of the latter category. I've always had the sense that something fundamental between my body and my soul was disconnected, like a very important wire got cut at some point, like my body is off on its own, doing its own thing, lazy and undependable.

But I have also long held the belief that one's tears are a guide, that when something makes you cry, it means something. If we pay attention to our tears, they'll show us something about ourselves. Against my preferences, watching people cross marathon finish lines makes me cry. Crazy deep ugly cry. Specifically, watching average-looking people cross marathon finish lines makes me cry. Professionals who finish in two hours are amazing, but it doesn't move me the same way. And not all physical feats move me like marathons do. I don't cry when I watch the Olympics or the Super Bowl. There's a thing I have with marathons.

Several friends and my brother ran the Chicago Marathon a few years ago, and I finally said out loud, "Sometime in my life I'm going to do that. Really. Me." I decided that in two years, I'd be ready. I'd be thirty-five; we'd celebrate our tenth wedding anniversary; Henry would be five—and it would be the perfect time to work off that baby weight after giving birth to the baby I was sure I was just about to conceive.

You see where this is going, of course. I want so badly to release my stranglehold on my plan, my way, my calendar. I want to be the kind of Christian who really does believe God holds the future and that even my best guesses are just that. I want to live without anxiety, fear, and deadlines. But it seems that every chance I get, I grab back those pretend reins and allow myself to believe the myth that I'm in control.

So I emailed a bunch of friends: *Two years from now—how about it? Let's do this!* There were, however, two problems with my plan. The first, of course, is that it was all based on my assumptions of how life would be. The second is that it was far enough away to not have to think about it for a long, long time.

That month I found out I was pregnant with twins. Delight, gratitude, hope. And an hour before I gave the eulogy at my grandmother's funeral, my doctor called with bad test results. Ultrasound, blood test, more ultrasounds, more blood tests. They knew at the beginning of the week that one baby was gone, and by the end of the week, the other was gone too. I don't remember very much from that week, except that my mom and my mother-in-law took great care of Henry as I dove into novel after novel to escape the plot twists of my own story.

As with anything devastating and medical, for a little while the world stops, but inevitably it must start again, and just after my world started again, when I started returning emails and shopping for groceries and doing the preschool drop-off again, I got an email from my friend Nate. Registration for the upcoming year's Chicago Marathon was open, he said. Was I still up for it? I immediately wrote a reply: No, not this year. *Next year.* And as soon as I wrote it, I knew it would always be my answer: *next year, next year, next year.* I deleted those words and began again.

Yes, I replied, before I could change my mind. Yes. I'm signing up. And I did. And then I dug out my running shoes—shoes that had been to the coffee shop and the farmers market but had never been running. I put on those shoes and shuffled around our neighborhood. It was March, less than seven months till the race. I sent an email to my friends—Nate was already signed up, and Jennifer, Kirsten, Deirdre, Blaine, and Margaret signed up too.

We all signed up to run with Team World Vision. Our family has sponsored a child through World Vision for years, and the money raised by Team World Vision runners buys wells and water purification systems for villages in Africa.

Training began in April, and I was incredibly nervous for our first group run. It was a three-mile timed run, and three miles was the upper edge of my limit. Also, the runners themselves kind of freaked me out. There was an uncomfortable amount of high fiving and slogan exchanging. The atmosphere was all very happy and motivational, and I wanted to hide. Every time someone mentioned a ten-mile run or a twenty-mile run with glee and anticipation, my stomach dropped. And then they'd say some clever running cliché, like, *If you can get to the starting line, you can get to the finish line.* That didn't seem remotely true and didn't help at all.

But I went back the next week and the next week and the next. And I began to understand what drove the acronyms and slogans and the almost violent positivity: you need it, that kind of enthusiasm, to get you up that early, to prod you along those miles. My life began to take on a new shape and rhythm. During the week I ran in the evenings, often with my dad and Aaron after work. Sometimes I ran before taking Henry to preschool. I showered and did stinky laundry all the time. I could tell you every detail about every house in our neighborhood, and every turn of the trail near our house.

Little by little, I began to think like a runner. I shopped for comfortable sports bras and wicking fabrics instead of ridiculous heels and sundresses. I began drinking water obsessively and found that especially after long runs I craved heaping bowls of salad, like The Green Well's Michigan Harvest Salad—greens, dried cherries, goat cheese, pears, walnuts, red grapes. I couldn't get enough of that salad, thick with fruit and cheese and nuts, more a dense, flavorful meal than a dainty plate of greens.

Over the months, my body got stronger and the miles got easier. At one point a friend said, "Whoa, Shauna, you have runner's calves." It may have been the best day of my life. I went to bed early on nights before long runs and watched what I ate and drank on those days.

What was interesting to me is that I found almost every runner I talked to had their own little cures and practices—no dairy before they run, lucky socks, a particular cup or particular kind of instant oatmeal. Marathon runners are nothing if not routine oriented and more than a little superstitious. I'm neither, generally, but the process rubbed off on me, and I found myself setting out my clothes the night before a run, getting a little funny about the contents of my fuel belt. Really, all you need to know is that I willingly wore a fanny pack and willingly referred to it as my "fuel belt."

Every Saturday, the Team World Vision runners showed up under the tender, brightening sky, nervous and sleepy. And we ran and talked and ran and talked. We learned one another's stories and secrets and idiosyncrasies. It's amazing what you'll say out loud at mile 15, when no one's looking you in the eye. It's all side by side, mile after mile, hour after hour, and the miles act like some sort of truth serum. You talk about chafing and rashes and digestive abnormalities, and then someone tells the story of how she got sober, or what it was like when his mother died. It's all out there, with nothing but the drumbeat of your feet and the rhythm of your ragged breath and the green of the trees on the path.

Each week of the summer the miles got longer—ten miles, sixteen miles, twenty miles. Each week I was surprised at what my body could do, this body I'd long suspected, squared off against, blamed. In the same way that giving birth had connected me to my body in a new and meaningful way, the training gave me a new respect for my body, for what it could do, for how strong and powerful it was.

Sometimes as I ran, I prayed for the people who would benefit from clean water as a result of the money we were raising. I'm generally a terrible fund-raiser, and in most situations I'd just end up writing a check so I didn't have to go through the awkwardness of asking people to give me money. I had no trouble, though, asking for money on behalf of Team World Vision. I wrote letters and made phone calls, and as I ran, I prayed for mothers and fathers and children half a world away whose lives could change as a result of access to clean water. On the longest, hottest training runs, our coaches reminded us to stay hydrated and encouraged us to pray every time we opened our water bottles, to let the clean, cool water that waited for us at every break become a symbol of the reason we were running. Especially on muggy summer mornings, water is a basic and necessary part of training, and it felt natural to thank God for clean water, and at the same time to thank him for allowing us to be part of providing clean water half a world away to men and women and children just like us, people exactly as thirsty as we are, people who need access to clean water just as fundamentally as we do.

Several members of the group I trained with and planned to run with dropped out one after another during the summer—a broken bone, an emergency surgery, a pregnancy, an injured knee. Kirsten, my patron saint of running, was my last hope, but when I talked with her the week of the race, she told me that a new job and a move and a crazy schedule hadn't allowed her to train. She was still flying in from San Francisco as planned, but she wasn't going to run. I drove to the city alone on Saturday, the day before the race, nervous to the point of tears, not sure who I'd run with, not sure how I'd make it without the drumbeat of my friends' feet on either side of me at the race the next day.

Kirsten met me at the hotel, and I don't know if she'd already changed her mind and decided to run since I'd talked to her last, or if she made the decision when she saw my panicky eyes, but in any case, she ended up joining me for every step of the race—my guide, my sister, my much-needed partner.

The race was all the things you think it will be: hard, boring, emotional, long, euphoric. The first thirteen miles were absolutely fun—as everyone says, Boystown is the best section of the Chicago Marathon: costumes, music, choreography, unbelievable people-watching. There were lots of friends along the way in that stretch—Jen's husband, Chris; my friend Jenny; Aaron's cousins. And then at the half-marathon turn, Aaron was there with our dear friends Jon and Christina, a great surprise, since I didn't think I'd see him till the finish line.

Just before the 14-mile mark, my knee and hip started to hurt so badly that I got scared. My hip had been sore since mile 3, and I'd been having trouble with my knee, on and off, for the last few weeks. I got a little panicky, but Kirsten told me to take some Advil and give it until mile 16. She was right—by 16 it was fine. We saw our friends Li-Pei, Sarah, and John, and then Aaron and his cousins again, and their faces gave us the energy we needed during the boring, treeless middle stretch.

For an October day in Chicago, the weather was crazy-hot, and at one point, Kirsten and I decided to speak only in clichés —"There's no I in TEAM." "If you get to the starting line, you can get to the finish line." "One foot in front of the other." "Trust your training." Those long miles between 16 and 22 weren't horrible or traumatic—just hard and hot and boring. The miles after the halfway point and before Chinatown are laborious, with no trees, no shade, thinner crowds. I started to get a little emotional about the finish at about mile 18, and Kirsten said, "Way too early for that, sister. Save it up."

The course takes you so far south of the finish line that you can't imagine you're ever going to get back up to Grant Park, so when we finally made the blessed turn at 35th Street, I told Kirsten I was both a little disoriented and kind of angry.

And then you hit mile 24, and you realize, *We're doing this. We're really going to do this.* You make the turn onto the bridge at Roosevelt, and you hear the announcer saying, "You're a part of Chicago Marathon history! You're not just a runner; you're a finisher, you're a marathoner!" People were screaming and Lake Michigan was so impossibly blue, and Kirsten and I both burst into tears and ran the last straightaway as fast as our busted-up legs could manage.

I tend to believe the worst about myself—I could never do this, I'm not that kind of person, I'll always be like this, or I'll never be able to get over that. But then I think about that day, and more than that, that season. I think about the miles on the green trail early in the morning and the taste of red Gatorade and the way my legs felt after those long runs. I think about the hushed, tense city the morning of the race as I walked over in near-darkness, all the runners wound up and silent, kicking out their legs over and over and pinning on their bibs. I think about the day after the race, when Kirsten and I hobbled around our neighborhood, sore and tired and proud of ourselves. And I remember that people can change. That I can change. That the same old refrains can get rewritten, and that all it takes sometimes is paying attention to your tears, and ignoring that voice that tries to hypnotize us with *next year, next year, next year.*

Green Well Salad

This is my take on The Green Well's Michigan Harvest Salad. The Green Well is one of my favorite Grand Rapids restaurants, and I've made this salad for dinner with roasted chicken in it, or for lunch with cheese and bread, or alongside the Real Simple Cassoulet for a homey, flavorful meal. The salad recipe calls for candied walnuts, but that's a touch too sweet for me, so I leave them unadorned, but toasting them for a minute is definitely a nice touch. One practical thought: I like to caramelize the onions earlier in the day so I'm not starving for salad and getting all impatient with how long the onions are taking.

One of my favorite meals of this year was a late lunch with my editors Angela and Carolyn. They flew in from Jackson, Mississippi, and Eugene, Oregon, respectively, and when they arrived at my house, before we started working, we ate lunch at the little round table in our living room— Green Well Salad, Irish cheese, crusty whole grain bread, sparkling water, and a little plate of coconut macaroons.

Ingredients

1 pound mixed greens

2 onions, thinly sliced

1 tablespoon butter

2 sliced pears

2 cups red grapes, halved

1 cup dried cherries, chopped if they're the big kind

1 cup walnuts, chopped

1 4-ounce container crumbled goat cheese

Maple vinaigrette:

1 tablespoon maple syrup

1 tablespoon Dijon

¼ cup balsamic vinegar

½ cup olive oil

   Salt and pepper to taste

Instructions

Begin by caramelizing the onions. Slice them thinly and cook them on medium-low heat in a tablespoon of butter until rich, dark brown, about 45 minutes.

For the vinaigrette:

Spoon Dijon into the bottom of a jelly jar. Add balsamic and maple syrup, salt, and pepper. Shake well. Add oil, and shake again. Taste and adjust for seasoning. Set aside.

For the salad:

Toss the greens with half the vinaigrette, then add the rest of the ingredients, the rest of the dressing, and toss again.

If you'd like to make it a more substantial main-course salad, you can add two cups or so of sliced, cooked chicken as well.

SERVES: 4 to 6

hummingbird

Aaron and I stopped "trying" to have a baby, because it was making me crazy and breaking my heart. I needed to get off that hamster wheel for a while, because I felt dizzy and all scraped away on the inside. I finally made an appointment with the doctor to talk about the next steps, more invasive steps, but the appointment was a long way off.

For no good reason, one dark morning, I took a pregnancy test. The pregnancy-test people have a racket going because of people like me, crazed and desperate enough to take a test about every six minutes for absolutely no reason, just in case we've gotten pregnant somehow since the last test, or just in case the last twenty-four tests were wrong. For a while, taking a pregnancy test was about as routine as brushing my teeth.

I found that each time a test was negative, it stopped the dreaming and hoping for a while. Taking the test was a way of puncturing the balloons of hope, because if I didn't, they would lift and lift without any evidence, and their falling back down every month was too painful. Essentially, I took all these tests to keep myself from hoping, because the hoping was breaking my heart.

But that morning, very early, the test was positive. Bright blue, unquestionably positive. I woke Aaron up out of a dead sleep. This is where our story becomes one of the clichés that made me so angry along the way. It didn't seem real, and the first two things I said were, "Thank you, God," and, "This is such a cliché."

Approximately one million and one people had suggested to me that when I stopped thinking about it and worrying about it, it would happen. That's sort of like telling someone who's up to bat not to worry about watching the ball, that the hit will come when you stop staring at the ball. Really? You know what will happen when you take your eye off the ball? At best, a strikeout; at worst, a serious head injury. It's like telling someone who's drowning to relax and let the water do its work. I know how that one ends. It's incredibly infuriating to be told to stop caring about something in order to make that very important thing happen.

And yet. And yet it's what happened for me, and for so many of my friends, and for enough other people for the cliché to arise. We had stopped "trying." No more counting days, no more schedule. I couldn't do the math anymore. And another cliché—I had made the appointment with the doctor to talk about fertility next steps. Everyone knows someone who, as soon as they made the appointment, found themselves pregnant. Basically at this point, based on the evidence I've seen, if I ever try to get pregnant again, I'm not going to pay attention to anything at all, and I'll also make a doctor's appointment. That should do it.

When I found out I was pregnant with Henry, I felt delight. But this time, one split second after the deep happiness, what I felt was fear. I basically wanted to be put into a bubble with a twenty-four-hour ultrasound so that I could always know if the baby was OK. I was so happy, and I was so scared. I prayed, but mostly in a manic way, almost chanting out loud, *please, please, please.* When I went to get my blood work done, I cried as I sat in the waiting room, not because I mind having blood drawn, but because it had been so long since I'd been to that doctor's office for anything but bad news, and because my nerves were wound so tightly the fear and anxiety leaked out of my eyes. After the miscarriages, I'm one of those patients who drives doctors and nurses crazy, because I know too much about the dark side of this. I know what *we'll see* means, and what *hmm* means, during an ultrasound. Worst of all, I know what silence signals. Silence is always, always bad.

The nurse just wanted to take my blood, but I wanted to review with her the things we were looking for in that particular draw. I rattled off the miscarriage details, the weeks, the kinds, the tests, the approximate levels of beta and progesterone we should have been looking for at that point. As though she didn't know. As though she could tell me anything from the vials of blood she drew as I talk-vomited my numbers and fears.

My cousin Melody was pregnant as well, after one healthy child and three miscarriages. One night, when we were all gathered around our table, another friend asked me if I was feeling nervous, and I redirected the question to Mel, who was almost thirty weeks along. "Well, I'm nervous, of course, but I'm sure it will get better. Mel, when did it get better for you?"

She didn't bat an eye. "I wish I could tell you something different, but I'm scared every single day. We know too much. We know what can happen."

She's right. With each of the last three pregnancies, I was ready to celebrate from the first moment, practically. With Henry, it was easy—everything about it. Easy to get pregnant, easy to stay pregnant, easy to deliver. I assumed the same for the second pregnancy and was shocked when the ultrasound showed a serious problem. The third time I was only nervous until we ruled out another molar pregnancy. Once we did, I didn't consider any other kind of problem.

But this time, I found myself worrying, praying, counting the days, thankful at the end of each day that I stayed pregnant one more day. Every day that passed with no bleeding, with no pain, felt like a gift. The first time I woke up nauseous, I was thrilled.

Our parents wanted to talk about names right away, to bring him or her into the family right away. But I needed test results, and an ultrasound, and another one after that. I needed days and weeks. Maybe months.

I was so desperately thankful, and so desperately scared. On one hand, I had made it through the loss of a pregnancy before. I knew I could make it through again. But at the same time, the mourning, the physical pain, the healing, the waiting, the trying again seemed more than I could imagine. And so I chanted my prayers over and over, and when I lay in bed at night, I chanted my gratitude for one more day. It was all I could do. It wasn't a baby yet, in my heart, but more like a promise, something that might be real, but wasn't real yet.

The doctors gave me lots of extra appointments and a ludicrous amount of ultrasounds. They assured me everything was fine. On Valentine's Day, we went to Table Fifty-Two, Art Smith's restaurant in the city, with good friends. His restaurant feels more like a home than a restaurant, in the very best way, and we had amazing goat cheese biscuits in a little cast-iron pan, fried chicken, and hummingbird cake. We laughed and told stories and watched a couple get engaged. I drank homemade ginger soda and rested my hands on my belly beneath the table *life, life, life*, smaller than a hummingbird.

And then the next morning, blood. In a split second, the door of my heart swung shut and locked like the door to a safe, impenetrable. An ultrasound showed a hemorrhage. It felt so incredibly familiar. I'd had so many more bad appointments than good, and while the good ones were nice while they lasted, the bad appointments were familiar. There was a 50 percent chance that the hemorrhage would diminish. That left a 50 percent chance that the hemorrhage would grow, and that the baby would not survive.

For me, fifty-fifty may as well have been zero-zero. I began to mourn. I knew how this story would end. One year earlier, almost to the day, I visited the same doctor for the same reason. One year earlier, almost to the day, I was bleeding, mourning the loss of one twin, waiting for results about the other. The news about the other was, of course, bad news. I couldn't imagine things being different this time.

My husband and my parents reminded me that fifty-fifty is good, but I couldn't get there. I asked for help and prayer from a couple of close friends because I couldn't pray with any feeling or belief. While I was mourning, they were praying on my behalf. I was so thankful for the prayers of our community—for people who prayed with faith and expectancy and courage when all I felt was fear and dread. I should have been praying, and I was, but they were the ragged, desperate prayers, their fabric torn with anger and shot through with bullets of accusation and bad memories. The prayers I prayed were rags, falling apart and dirty, stained with all of my bad memories of what feels like the same terrible thing all over again.

The doctor said there was nothing to do but wait, and that while it probably wouldn't make a difference, the less activity on my part, the better. If I was too active, the hemorrhage could injure the baby. That was all I needed to hear. I planted myself on the couch and didn't leave for weeks. I would have done anything for this baby, and though a doctor friend told me that doctors recommend bed rest mostly so wound-up pregnant women can feel like they're contributing in some way, even if medically it won't make much of a difference, I didn't care. I bed rested like a champion. I would have gold medaled in the bed rest Olympics.

Our friends brought flowers and soup and enchiladas. They stopped over and texted and helped with Henry.

My friend Emily, who was also pregnant, came to keep me company on the couch one weekend, and then an ice storm in her hometown kept her at our house for several wonderful, funny extra days. We spent what seemed like a thousand hours in our living room, reading magazines and watching movies and eating takeout, coloring with Henry. Sometimes we talked about the fear, about the bleeding, about the baby, but sometimes we talked about fashion and marriage and memories we've all made at the lake. She was still in town for my follow-up appointment, and she met me at the door when I got home, tears in her eyes, nervous.

Very good news, I told her. Best possible news. The hemorrhage diminished. Everything was fine. I couldn't believe it. The doctor said she'd never seen a hemorrhage diminish so quickly. Emily and I cried and hugged around our pregnant bellies, and then we persuaded Kristi to meet us for lunch at Francesca's for pizzas and pastas and bread and cheese, a celebration of good news and hope and relief.

Our little hummingbird was still beating its tiny wings, and even though my fear was detonating over and over like bombs dropping, the fragile and fractured wings of my heart dared to beat as well, and alongside all that fear and all that gratitude, I felt the first precious rush of hope.

Goat Cheese Biscuits

At Table Fifty-Two, Art Smith's charming restaurant, these biscuits are served instead of bread before the meal. They're rich and buttery and tangy, and when I make them, I serve them with strawberry jam—the perfect breakfast, or a lovely thing to serve with sparkling wine as dinner guests are arriving.

The original recipe calls for self-rising flour and buttermilk, two things I don't tend to keep in the house. But on a dreary Saturday morning, I was aching to try them. I had the goat cheese and the cast-iron skillet, and I was determined to make it work. I substituted a mix of flour, baking powder, and salt for the self-rising flour, and plain yogurt for the buttermilk, and the biscuits were just delicious. Now I make them that way every time.

Ingredients

- 2 cups flour
- 3 teaspoons baking powder
- 2 teaspoons salt
- 1 cup plain yogurt
- 6 tablespoons cold butter, divided
- 4 tablespoons goat cheese, crumbled
- ¼ cup Parmesan cheese, grated

Instructions

Preheat oven to 425 degrees and place a 10-inch cast-iron pan into the oven while it's preheating.

Pour flour, baking powder, and salt into a medium-sized bowl. Cut 4 tablespoons of the butter into small pieces and add it to the bowl, with the goat cheese and the yogurt. Stir until the mix is moistened, adding an extra tablespoon of yogurt if needed.

Remove the hot skillet from the oven and place a tablespoon of butter into it. When the butter has melted, divide the batter into 12 biscuits, each about the size of a golf ball, and then nestle them into the pan—they'll be snuggled in there pretty cozily, and that's all right. I usually start by making a ring of 9 around the edge, then 3 in the middle.

Brush the tops of the biscuits with one tablespoon of melted butter. Bake for 14 to 16 minutes until browned on the top and bottom. Remove from the oven and sprinkle with the grated Parmesan cheese.

MAKES: one dozen biscuits

Conversions:

1 cup self-rising flour = 1 cup flour, 1½ teaspoons baking powder, ½ teaspoon salt
1 cup buttermilk = 1 cup plain yogurt

part two

You say grace before meals.
All right.
But I say grace before the concert and the opera,
And grace before the play and pantomime,
And grace before I open a book,
And grace before sketching, painting,
Swimming, fencing, boxing, walking, playing, dancing
And grace before I dip the pen in the ink.

G. K. CHESTERTON, "A Grace," *Collected Poetry*

delicious everywhere

One of the best parts of my childhood was traveling with my dad. He spent most of his work time at our church, preaching and leading the staff, but sometimes he traveled to other churches, meeting with pastors to talk about faith and leadership and the great privilege that it is for ordinary people to be a part of God's story being written on earth. When I was in elementary school, he took me all over the country. In junior high and high school, I went with him to France, Spain, and Germany, to India and Australia.

He worked long hours on those trips, and while he worked, I explored and ate. We'd have breakfast together at the hotel, and he'd give me a challenge for the day. He'd say, "OK, Sydney is known for seafood, so tonight I want to have dinner with you at the best sushi restaurant you can find." He'd say, "Find out what the locals eat in Málaga," or, "Choose a great dinner place in Frankfurt."

I experienced so many cities by myself, wandering markets and shops, museums and parks. I loved the challenge of figuring out a city's public transportation system, and delighted in discovering new neighborhoods and eavesdropping on people at cafés. People are sometimes horrified when they hear that I wandered so many big cities all alone as a young teenager, but I found that people all over the world were charming and helpful, and that there might not be as much to fear as we think. I did get my wallet stolen once, but without violence, and I hope our children find the world to be as big and wonderful as I do because of the travel I was able to do at a relatively young age.

The challenges my dad gave me weren't always food-related. On one trip to Europe, I was the only young person and the only female with a group of my dad's colleagues. I asked them what they'd gotten for their wives, since we'd return to Chicago on Valentine's Day. They stared at me blankly and wordlessly handed me cash. I bought all sorts of charming, romantic presents in southern Spain. They were relieved, and I had a fantastic time picking out jewelry and tiny vases and scarves.

Now, it seems, it's entirely possible to travel without tasting a new culture, should you desire to do so. There's a McDonald's practically everywhere, and you can just as easily find a bottle of Coke in the bush in Uganda as on Michigan Avenue. But when I traveled with my dad, he taught me that wherever we are, we eat what they eat, and we eat what they give us, all the time. We taste the place when we eat what our hosts eat. As we traveled, food became a language for understanding, even more so than museums or history lessons.

My memories of the places I've visited locate themselves almost entirely in my senses, particularly in my tastes and smells. Málaga, on the southern coast of Spain, was the spicy, garlicky soup full of shells and fish that our hosts served to us at almost midnight, and the smell of brandy that the men drank on the balcony after dinner. India was strong, sweet tea; flaky rice; warm naan dripping with butter; mango juice and custard. Nairobi was whole grilled fish and tall bottles of Orange Fanta. Paris was café au lait and baguettes. I remember those places with my mouth and my tongue and my nose, and still now I'll smell something and it will take me right back to a faraway place, to Bath or Berlin or Bethlehem.

In college, I spent most of a fall semester in England, Ireland, and Scotland. Our time in Britain was amazing—the theater! The literature! The history! The food, though, was a little less spectacular. I know the London food scene is thriving now, that there are fantastic restaurants rewriting British food's dismal reputation, but this was before that. Also, we had no money and were fed largely by nuns who ran the fifteenth-century manor house we lived in. They were great at stretching ingredients, and slightly less great, shall we say, at flavoring them.

When we were "home" at the manor house, we'd have boiled vegetables for lunch, and then those same vegetables would find themselves in a soup at dinner. We forced ourselves to finish the soup, because we feared seeing that same poor vegetable in yet another form. When we ate out, because we were in college, we bought drinks first, of course, and with any leftover cash, bought soggy fried fish or sandwiches that were mostly mayonnaise. It was not a rich culinary season, for the most part.

And then Israel. At the end of the semester, in December, we landed in Tel Aviv late at night. The air was warm and our hotel was right on the water, so we dropped our bags in our rooms and went swimming in our clothes, waves crashing under the black sky. The next morning, our first meal there was nothing short of a revelation.

Our hosts had laid out platters of hummus and olives, egg salad and tomatoes, figs and honey. After so many months of being inside, in the rain, in the clouds, in dreary and damp pubs, on that morning we were outside, and the air was warm and dry. It smelled like olives, and the food was fresh and simple and beautiful. It tasted like the sun, like the earth, like the food that people have been eating in that place for a thousand years, because that's what it was.

In Italy the summer before Henry was born, on a trip with family friends, we ate raw green olives in Positano, looking out at the Mediterranean Sea, and we drank Bellinis made with thick white peach puree. We ate paper-thin pizzas with narrow ribbons of basil and fried zucchini blossoms stuffed with ricotta, impossibly rich and light at once.

On that trip I had the best meal of my life, on the island of Capri, at a restaurant called da Paolina's Lemon Tree. Our family and friends sat at a round table, and the branches of the lemon trees hung so low and so thick they almost made a ceiling, a dense canopy over our heads, while hundreds of lanterns hung from their branches and made the whole dining area twinkle as they swayed.

Our table had a whole fish roasted with wheels of lemon and swaths of herbs, carved tableside, and handmade lobster ravioli, the fresh lobster meat so sweet that it almost tasted like there was sugar in it. What moved me, though—and what the restaurant is famous for beyond the lemon tree canopy—were the antipasti and sweet buffets: two huge wood tables piled heavily with platters wedged in like puzzle pieces. One table held cheeses and pastas and grilled, marinated vegetables; the other, plates of every imaginable fruit, cake, and tart. At the center of that lovely table, a bowl of fat blackberries, almost as big as plums, and a bowl of whipped cream, decadent and simple at once.

I can still taste the tiny glass of limoncello they served at the end of the meal, and I can still recall the hint of coolness in the air as we drove back down the winding roads to the marina, feeling like the world was so beautiful I almost couldn't stand it, so thankful for those trees and those lanterns and those huge round tables and that bowl of blackberries.

On my thirty-fifth birthday, we sat around a table with dear friends overlooking the harbor in Edgartown on Martha's Vineyard. We had lunch at the Atlantic, where we shared bowls of hot, salty truffle fries, and I had a watermelon feta salad with arugula and mint, the shards of feta rich and tangy against the sweetness of the watermelon.

As night fell, we went to Oak Bluffs for the Grand Illumination at the gingerbread cottages. The gingerbread cottages are tiny, ornate, brightly painted cottages in a winding narrow-streeted neighborhood in the middle of Oak Bluffs, and in the center of the neighborhood is an open-air pavilion, the site of Methodist revivals since the Civil War. On the night of the Grand Illumination, people gather outside the pavilion on blankets and beach towels, and when the program is done, all at once, all the gingerbread cottages light their lanterns. The tiny neighborhood glows with hundreds of lanterns, and people walk up and down the narrow streets, picking their favorites, greeting neighbors and old friends.

I'd been warned that thirty-five can be a rough birthday, and I had myself steeled for it. But as we took the ferry back to Cape Cod, the twinkling lights of Oak Bluffs receding, the stars burning bright and reflecting on the water, I felt so thankful I could have wept. I sat near the ferry's railing, the beauty of the lanterns and the taste of tangy feta against sweet watermelon still on my tongue.

I hold all these places and flavors with me, like a fistful of shiny coins, like a charm bracelet. I want to be everywhere at once. I want a full English breakfast at a pub in London, and hot buttery naan in New Delhi for lunch. I want conch fritters at a beach bar in the Bahamas, and an ice-cold Fanta overlooking Lake Victoria. I want Cowgirl Creamery's Triple Creme Brie at the Ferry Plaza Farmers Market in San Francisco, and the gingerbread pancakes from Magnolia Cafe in Austin. I want it all—all the tastes, all the smells, all the stories and memories and traditions, all the textures and flavors and experiences, all running down my chin, all over my fingers.

Sometimes people ask me why I travel so much, and specifically why we travel with Henry so often. I think they think it's easier to keep the kids at home, in their routines, surrounded by their stuff. It is. But we travel because it's there. Because Capri exists and Kenya exists and Tel Aviv exists, and I want to taste every bite of it. We travel because I want my kids to learn, as I learned, that there are a million ways to live, a million ways to eat, a million ways to dress and speak and view the world. I want them to know that "our way" isn't the right way, but just one way, that children all over the world, no matter how different they seem, are just like the children in our neighborhood—they love to play, to discover, to learn.

I want my kids to learn firsthand and up close that different isn't bad, but instead that different is exciting and wonderful and worth taking the time to understand. I want them to see themselves as bit players in a huge, sweeping, beautiful play, not as the main characters in the drama of our living room. I want my kids to taste and smell and experience the biggest possible world, because every bite of it, every taste and texture and flavor, is delicious.

Watermelon Feta Salad

Ingredients

- 8 cups watermelon, cubed
- 8 ounces feta cheese, crumbled
- 3 tablespoons fresh mint, chopped
- ¼ of a red onion, finely chopped
- 10 ounces arugula
- 2 limes
- ¼ cup white balsamic vinegar or white wine vinegar
- ½ cup olive oil
- Salt and pepper to taste

Instructions

Cube 8 cups of watermelon, and let the cubes marinate in the juice of one fresh squeezed lime for several hours.

Vinaigrette:

Combine fresh squeezed lime juice and zest from the remaining lime, white balsamic vinegar or white wine vinegar, olive oil, salt, and pepper.

At serving time, toss arugula with half the vinaigrette, and combine watermelon, feta, red onion, and fresh mint. Layer the watermelon mixture over the arugula, and drizzle with remaining vinaigrette.

SERVES: 6 to 8

jazz and curry

I'm not really a recipe girl. My mom always teases me about it, knowing that when I say I used a recipe, all it means is that at some point, some list of ingredients and techniques were involved as I threw things in pans, as I sliced, poured, salted, and peppered with seeming randomness. She does not particularly appreciate this cooking style, and sometimes she has to leave the kitchen because my loosey-goosey approach makes her nervous.

There are, of course, some times when recipes are more important than others. When you're baking bread, for example, if you were to decide the yeast wasn't important, you'd have something between pita and a paper plate. In cooking as in life, there are some nonnegotiables, but not nearly as many as you think. Learning to cook is all about learning those nonnegotiables and then playing around with the rest. Recipes are how we learn all the rules, and cooking is knowing how to break them to suit our tastes or preferences. Following a recipe is like playing scales, and cooking is jazz.

In one of my favorite *Food & Wine* articles, Daniel Duane writes about cooking with Thomas Keller of the French Laundry in Napa Valley.[1] Keller is, of course, one of the great American chefs, known for his obsessive pursuit of perfection and fanatical attention to detail. You can imagine, then, that when Daniel Duane had the opportunity to cook the chef's recipes with the chef himself, he was expecting to be instructed on the tiniest of details.

Instead, though, Keller told him to make the recipe once according to the instructions. The second time, he told Duane to rewrite the recipe in his own terms, adjusting for his taste, cutting out or adding steps according to what made sense to him. The third time, Keller said to make it without any recipe at all, just by his memory and tastes and hands. And at that point, he said, "The recipe is yours."

I adore this approach. This makes sense to me. Recipes are the scales, the training wheels, the paint-by-numbers that lead us to jazz, two-wheel riding, and our very own blank canvas.

We learn by doing, and there's no way around it. There is no stand-in for standing in your own kitchen, a trial by fire, literally. You can buy it in a box; you can watch someone else make it for you on TV. But there's no replacement for what happens when we make something with our own hands, directed by our own senses, motivated by our own love for the people we're serving.

I first made Sally Sampson's chicken curry with mangoes ten years ago. And since then I think I've made it a thousand times, a thousand ways. I've served it to children and grandparents, at lunch parties and holiday dinners. There are countless curry recipes, some more authentic than others. I'm not making a case for the fact that a woman named Sally Sampson has the most authentic Indian curry recipe to be found, and I know that more serious cooks prefer not to use the blended spice mix of curry but instead like to make their own. But I'm telling you this is a delicious curry, my very favorite.

It's fabulous reheated, can be stretched for a crowd, and feels a little fancy, especially if you top it with lots of basil and cilantro and lime wedges around the edges. It's dairy-free and can easily be made gluten-free by dusting the chicken with brown rice flour instead of all-purpose. It's great with peaches if you can't find mangoes, and in a pinch once, instead of fresh mangoes I used canned ones that I found in a little marina shop in the British Virgin Islands. Also there, I used bone-in, skin-on chicken because that's the only way we could buy it, and that worked too.

I've served this to picky extended family members and several of Aaron's bands over the years, and our friend Steve has requested it for his birthday several years running. I made it for an engagement dinner recently, and that night our friend Mark ate so many helpings that his wife, Courtney, scolded him, and also asked for the recipe.

I made it for Annette and Andrew's first and last meal in our Grand Rapids home — the first time they visited and at their good-bye dinner when they moved home to California. Years ago, on their way from Paris to San Diego, which was home for them at the time, they stopped to see us in Grand Rapids. We were having a dinner party that night and expected them very late, after the party was over, but they arrived a little early. I left mid-meal to pick them up and then deposited them, fresh from an international flight, at our table. Our other guests had finished eating, so we cleared their plates and set out new ones for Annette and Andrew. We made introductions and poured more wine all around, and when I think of that night, it's one of my favorite memories, because they arrived right in the middle of a meal around our table, which is the way I'd like to arrive everywhere. And though we couldn't have predicted it then, a year later they moved to Grand Rapids and spent hundreds of nights around that same table.

So try it. Try Keller's three-times plan. Make it once according to the recipe. Then you know how the chef or recipe writer intended it to taste. Practice your scales. And then write your own version of the recipe. And then make it entirely from memory, at which point it's yours.

Mango Chicken Curry

Adapted from Sally Sampson's The $50 Dinner Party
(Simon & Schuster, 1998).

I do know that as far as recipes go, this looks like a hard one because it has such a long list of ingredients, but it's mostly just chopping and throwing things in. Allow yourself plenty of time to chop, but that's the extent of the difficulty. There are no tricky techniques involved, I promise.

I double the recipe for dinner parties of 10 to 12 people, and serve it with a very simple green salad and pita bread or naan. We're always glad for leftovers, because I think it might even be better the next day.

Ingredients

¼ cup flour
2 tablespoons curry powder
1 teaspoon sea salt
¼ teaspoon cayenne pepper
2½–3 pounds boneless, skinless chicken breasts, cut into small pieces
2–4 tablespoons olive oil
2 garlic cloves, chopped
1 red onion, chopped
1 tablespoon fresh ginger, chopped
1 red bell pepper, chopped
4 cups chicken broth
¼ cup currants or raisins
2 roma tomatoes, diced
1 mango, pitted and diced
1 tablespoon fresh lime juice
3 tablespoons fresh cilantro, chopped
3 tablespoons fresh basil, chopped

Instructions

Mix together flour, curry powder, salt, and cayenne pepper.

Toss chicken breast pieces into the flour mixture.

Add 1 to 2 tablespoons olive oil to a pan, and cook chicken on medium-high heat until browned, about 5 minutes on each side. Set aside.

Add additional 1 to 2 tablespoons olive oil and cook garlic, red onion, ginger, and red pepper until onion is golden, about 4 minutes.

Add chicken back to the pan, lower heat.

Add 4 to 4½ cups chicken broth.

Cook at a simmer until chicken is tender and broth is reduced by one-fourth.

Add currants, tomatoes, and mango, and simmer until heated through.

Off heat, add lime juice, cilantro, basil.

Serve over rice.

SERVES: 6

1. Daniel Duane, "Become an Intuitive Cook: Thomas Keller's Cooking Lessons," *Food & Wine*, December 2010, www.foodandwine.com/articles/become-an-intuitive-cook-thomas-kellers-cooking-lessons (accessed October 11, 2012).

open the door

It seems to me that women typically experience shame about two things: their bodies and their homes. Men, in my experience, have no such shame about their homes. Maybe for them it's about paychecks or cars or something, and these are stereotypes, but in our house, they hold true. Aaron will invite someone into our house and not even notice as they walk in that his socks are on the floor or that the dishes in the sink are spilling onto the counter on either side. He fails to see the cereal-and-milk smears on the table, the sticky spoon, the crumbs on the counter. Meanwhile, I consider lying to the people in our foyer about a gas leak or something, anything to get them back on to the porch so I can sprint around with baby wipes in one hand and a laundry basket in the other.

When we were first married, Aaron and I lived in a one-bedroom town house so small we couldn't both sit at our kitchen table at the same time, and the only place for his grand piano was in our bedroom. Let's be clear: that piano in the bedroom sounds more romantic than it is. It was mostly a really big piece of furniture on which to pile our clothes, but sometimes in the middle of the night, Aaron would terrify me out of a dead sleep by sneaking out of bed to play "Great Balls of Fire" at a shattering volume. In the basement, he had a recording studio and rehearsal space, and the high school students we worked with at the time trundled up and down those basement steps a thousand times, dragging guitars and amps and cymbals.

It was not perfect, and it was not fancy, but it was my own very first house, and then our first house together. I wanted so badly to fill it with laughter and memories and celebration that I willed myself to overlook what it lacked, and threw open the door at every opportunity.

In the years we lived in that tiny place, we must have had a hundred parties. We had dinner parties around our coffee table, a pillow for each person leaning back against the couch. In the summer, we'd grill out and fill a kiddie pool with ice and bottles of beer and soda, until our neighborhood association threatened to fine us for having a swimming facility without a fence. It seemed obvious to us that a kiddie pool full of ice cubes and beer wasn't really an invitation to swim, but that seemed beside the point.

We had a big Christmas party one year, and because the town house was so small, the only way to get everyone in and make sure they had access to food and drinks was to set up small stations of food and drinks in every room—ice buckets of champagne and tiny turkey sandwiches and little pots of sweet and spicy mustards on the coffee table and the kitchen counter, with another platter down in the studio, next to the drums, and another in the loft.

I realized that even those stations weren't enough, and that the only remaining space was our bedroom. Just before guests started arriving, I took a deep breath, shoved all of our clothes and shoes in the closet, and put a platter of sandwiches and an ice bucket with champagne on the piano. At one point in the night, I found a whole group of our friends lounging on our bed with sandwiches and champagne flutes. Later in the evening I found them trying on all of my shoes.

What people are craving isn't perfection. People aren't longing to be impressed; they're longing to feel like they're home. If you create a space full of love and character and creativity and soul, they'll take off their shoes and curl up with gratitude and rest, no matter how small, no matter how undone, no matter how odd.

When we moved to Grand Rapids, we lived in a big old charming English Tudor built in the 1920s. What we know now, by the way, is that *charm* is generally a euphemism for "wow, this place is about to fall down." It was charming in every sense, with slanted floors and built-in cabinets, radiators that clanked and light fixtures that blinked as though they were haunted. Every light switch and doorknob was from a different era, and the windows in the upstairs bathroom needed to be replaced so badly that an actual breeze fluttered the curtains even when the windows were shut tight.

We hosted holiday gatherings and barbecues, fancy dinner parties and poker nights. At one dinner party, a bat flew down from the attic and out through the dining room's french doors. The heating in the dining room was so uneven that we gave blankets to the people on the window side, while the people across the table glistened with sweat. And, of course, my memories of entertaining in that house are very sweet, bats and radiators notwithstanding. We made thousands of memories around that table, in the narrow kitchen, and on the back patio strung with lights.

These days we live in a little ranch that I love for the big windows and the simplicity of it, but we don't have space for a hundred. We have space for thirty—kind of, if I borrow silverware and chairs and people balance their plates on their laps and sit on the floor. So that's what we do. We throw open the front door and invite people into our home, despite its size, despite its imperfections. We practice hospitality, creating soft and safe places for people to connect and rest.

I really believed I had been making progress along the way on my house shame, until a friend stopped over unannounced recently. This friend happens to have a truly beautiful old home, the kind with a butler's pantry and a grand staircase, full of antiques and monogrammed silver frames and cashmere throws, different from our home in practically every way. She collects hotel silver and presses her napkins. I have never seen her home less than sparkling. Ever.

She came in and hugged me and sat on the couch in our kitchen, and we chatted about various things—her work, my work, our kids. And I tried not to absolutely freak out. I hope she didn't notice that I practically developed a facial tic while we chatted.

This is the thing: it was an unannounced stopover. While I was writing. When I'm writing at home, it's as though I am a homebound invalid. No makeup, hair in a ratty bun just above my forehead. Crooked glasses, Aaron's gym socks. I'm not suggesting I was just a little ragged around the edges; I was terrifying. My brother had given me a sailing shirt, one of those half-zips made of some sort of wicking fabric. I thought it would make me look a little sporty. I realized, though, after my friend left, that it does not make me look sporty; it makes me look like a forty-eight-year-old athletic director at a small women's college.

Let's talk for a moment about my home during that fateful visit. First, the smell: my whole house smelled because I hadn't done the dishes for days. Many, many days. There are reasons for this, of course, but when someone's standing in your kitchen, it's hard to explain the breakfast dishes on the coffee table, the popcorn bits all over the rug, and the smell—heavens, the smell!—of dirty dishes in the sink.

This is the shame double whammy—my body and my house. It was almost physically painful. But this is the thing: she's my friend. And even though having her sit right in the middle of my house mess set off every shame alarm I have, I stayed there, perched on my couch, listening and talking.

Just the week before, she and I had been talking about the writing I was doing, and I was telling her that while I'm writing about food, what I'm finding is that a lot of it is about shame, about the ways we feel inferior, and because of those feelings, we hide. And of course, it's all fun and games to talk about those ideas, and then the next thing you know, you're in your husband's gym socks and your kitchen stinks. You've got a chance to practice what you're preaching, and you're breaking out in hives.

I felt within myself the desire to shoo her out, to hide, to keep her from the disorder that is my real, actual life some days. But I took a deep breath, and she sat there listening to me across my dirty coffee table, and we talked about community and family and authenticity. It's easy to talk about it, and really, really hard sometimes to practice it.

This is why the door stays closed for so many of us, literally and figuratively. One friend promises she'll start having people over when they finally have money to remodel. Another says she'd be too nervous that people wouldn't eat the food she made, so she never makes the invitation.

But it isn't about perfection, and it isn't about performance. You'll miss the richest moments in life—the sacred moments when we feel God's grace and presence through the actual faces and hands of the people we love—if you're too scared or too ashamed to open the door. I know it's scary, but throw open the door anyway, even though someone might see you in your terribly ugly half-zip.

White Chicken Chili

This is one of those go-to dinners you can pretty much always throw together, perfect for last-minute guests. It's easy and quick, and all the ingredients are things you're likely to have on hand: frozen chicken breasts, canned beans, broth, jar of salsa—although fresh is better than jarred. Fresh from the store, I mean, like from the produce section. If you're making homemade salsa, that's fantastic, but you're in a different gear, certainly, than white chicken chili gear. By all means, make homemade salsa. But then definitely don't dump it in the chili. It would be both show-offy and sort of useless, like putting on makeup before bed.

This is what you make on cold, weary nights, nights when you're so worn through and chilled to the bone that the only thing that will cure you is something thick, spicy, and eaten with a spoon. And this is what you make when a quick stopover turns to dinner. Open the chips and the salsa, and let your guests begin crunching away while you start the chicken. You can even put them to work chopping cilantro and slicing limes.

A couple great things about this soup: first, it's gluten-free and dairy-free, things that are very important in our house. This is a good meal to bring to friends who just had a baby—warm, easy, comforting. Bring a big container of chili, with chips, salsa, cheese, avocado, etc.

And this is a perfect Sunday afternoon football meal—great with beer and big piles of chips. For crowds, I like serving both traditional beef chili and this one too—two big bubbling pots on the stove, the counter full of bowls of toppings for both.

This is a highly versatile recipe, like all my favorite recipes are. You can add a can of corn or even corn with peppers. You can use tomatillo salsa if you'd like, and a can of diced green chilis, and then it's chicken chili verde, which is lovely for a change. You could add a can of black beans if you'd like, for a little color and for their mineral-y, almost chocolate-y flavor. To make it even one step easier, you can use a rotisserie chicken, skin removed and meat shredded.

I wouldn't add kidney beans, because that would make it too much like a plain old chili, and because, to be honest with you, I don't like kidney beans. *There really aren't too many things I just don't like, but kidney beans are one. For the record: I also don't love ham, cinnamon, or white chocolate. But I digress ... back to the chili at hand.*

Serve with cilantro, wedges of lime, sliced avocado, shredded cheese, chips, sour cream, and salsa. I will warn you, however, that sometimes what began as a thoroughly virtuous soup becomes a very large meal consisting mainly of cheese and chips, with a very occasional bite of soup. Or at least that's what I've heard.

Ingredients

1–1½ pounds chicken—breasts, tenders, or boneless skinless thighs, cut into bite-sized pieces.

1 16-ounce container of salsa, preferably fresh. Or green salsa, as discussed above.

4 cans white beans

4 cups chicken broth

Instructions

In a dutch oven or stockpot, cook over medium heat until chicken is almost cooked through, about 5 minutes. Add salsa and beans, including bean liquid, and broth.

Bring to a rolling boil, then reduce heat to a simmer, stirring occasionally.

Simmer for at least 30 minutes, but, really, the longer the better.

SERVES: 6

baking cookies
with batman

The year after we were married, just after we moved to Grand Rapids, Aaron's body stopped healing itself, slowly at first, and then all at once.

One stormy, low-skyed night, when Aaron got back from church, he held his hands out to me and laid them, palms up, on my knees. The place where his thumb met his hand, the lower part of his palm, was black and blue, raised, hard as a rock, and the tendon that stretched from his wrist to his elbow was swollen and taut like a bone. He's a pianist, and little by little that year, his hands and elbows and wrists stopped working.

That night we stared at each other. What does a pianist do when his hands stop working? And his hands were just one part of it. He had the growing sense that his body wasn't healing itself the way it should, that when he got sick, he stayed sick longer than other people did, that small things flattened him with pain and exhaustion.

He asked everyone he knew what he should do about his hands. He went to doctor after doctor, and the answer was always the same: injections and surgery. Cut this; numb the pain with this; sever this; reposition this.

Several members of Aaron's family are chiropractors. They

are non-vaccinators, natural childbirth devotees, and home birth enthusiasts. He'd no sooner let a surgeon touch his hands than sever them completely off. This is one of the many differences between our families of origin. His family believes in non-FDA-approved herbal supplements and the importance of spinal alignment. My family believes in Advil and the healing effects of both red wine and boating.

Everyone he talked to was more concerned with the mechanical problem of his hands and wrists, and less concerned with the fact that his whole body seemed to be turning on itself. Surgery was the refrain, and with each passing month, Aaron grew both more desperate and more certain that a scalpel wasn't the solution.

A friend from our new church recommended a local doctor who practiced alternative medicine. The doctor was brilliant and articulate and passionate, and always wore an extremely dapper shirt-and-tie combo. Aaron and I both loved him right off the bat.

The doctor assessed quickly that the problem was inflammation, and that essentially, Aaron's body was working so hard to heal the inflammation caused on an ongoing basis by eating foods his body can't process that it was unable to heal other parts of his body, namely, his hands. The doctor put Aaron on a twenty-eight-day detox, removing all common allergens and all processed food. At the end of those twenty-eight days, Aaron felt better than he had in years. His hands and wrists were stronger and less painful than they had been in months.

What we learned over time is that Aaron's body doesn't tolerate gluten. When he eats it, his entire system rebels — stomach, throat, hands, wrists, mood, everything. And when he cuts out gluten, his body does all the things it should do. It heals and restores itself. He sleeps well. He sings well. He lives well. It really is that simple. Cutting out one food made all the difference for his hands and wrists.

I'm one of those people who was raised to eat everything. Eat what they give you; try everything; don't offend your host. Being low-maintenance about food was a family value growing up in my house. Because of this, I've been less than patient with people who have lots of "I don't eat this; I don't eat that" requirements. I used to grumble as I planned menus, trying to figure out some culinary silver bullet that would feed the gluten-free, the dairy-free, the nut-free, and the pescatarian.

I've learned so much, though, walking with Aaron through the fear about his hands and the fear of not being able to make music and the eventual solution, and that journey has given me a new vantage point on all this complicated eating. For Aaron, the relationship between how he eats and how he lives is direct. This is not a fiddly, high-maintenance fad for him. I wouldn't deny him medicine, of course. So why would I be difficult about the foods that heal him, and the ones that keep him sick?

The heart of hospitality is about creating space for someone to feel seen and heard and loved. It's about declaring your table a safe zone, a place of warmth and nourishment. Part of that, then, is honoring the way God made our bodies, and feeding them in the ways they need to be fed.

I do draw a line between food restrictions for health reasons and plain old picky eating. I bend over backward for the first —I make sure to have a meal that includes a filling and beautiful option for people who can't eat one or another part of the whole meal. I'm not much of a meat-eater myself, although I have no policies about it, so it's not much of a stretch to make sure there's something good for a vegetarian at my table.

What I don't do, though, is knock myself out for picky eaters. Part of eating at someone's table is learning about the tastes and textures and flavors of their home, and part of eating at someone's table is understanding that homes are not restaurants and your host is not a short-order cook.

When I first began cooking and hosting, I felt more pressure to work around each possible dislike or preference — serve this on the side, serve that three ways so everyone can have it their way. But, really, "have it your way" is a fast-food ad campaign, not a compelling rationale for how we should gather around one another's tables.

So this is the dance, it seems to me: to be the kind of host who honors the needs of the people who gather around his or her table, and to be the kind of guest who comes to the table to learn, not to demand.

Aaron doesn't have celiac disease, so we don't have to be super-super-vigilant about cooking in separate pans, but his sensitivity to gluten is pretty significant, so over the last ten years or so, this pasta- and bread-loving wife has become somewhat of an expert on gluten-free cooking and eating and living.

Our son, Henry, has always been an early, early, early riser. I dream about sleeping until 7:00 a.m., but most of the time, the day starts around 5:00. Aaron and I take turns getting up with him, and one of my favorite things to do with him is make gluten-free breakfast cookies and then take them to Aaron in bed with a coffee and a wriggly, snuggly boy.

When we bake, Henry turns a dining room chair around and pulls it up to the kitchen counter, and he lines up his guys so they can help too. Sometimes Batman and Aquaman, sometimes Wolverine, sometimes Optimus Prime and Megatron. It's his job to mash the bananas with a fork, and while I measure, he dumps in each ingredient. I scoop the batter onto the cookie sheet, and he pats it down with the back of a spoon.

When the cookies are baked and cooled, we put a little plate of them on a tray with a cup of coffee that has lots of warm almond milk in it. Henry runs in first, jumping on Aaron and wriggling his way under the covers with him, and I balance the tray on the nightstand before crawling in too.

Breakfast Cookies

This recipe is adapted from Nikki's Healthy Cookies, from Heidi Swanson's lovely blog, www.101cookbooks.com.

Heidi's recipe calls for chopped dark chocolate, cinnamon, and unsweetened coconut flakes. I reduce the amount of chocolate because it's breakfast, and the point of this cookie is that I want to feel deeply virtuous when I eat it in the morning, so I replace most of the chocolate with chopped walnuts. Also, forget what I just said about virtue, because I use sweetened coconut. It's the only kind I can get without a trip to Whole Foods, which isn't always part of our weekly routine. The sweetened coconut makes the cookie sweeter, obviously, so you don't miss the chocolate as much. And I omit the cinnamon, because, as I've already confessed, I don't really like cinnamon.

Also, Heidi makes sweet little cookies, little bites almost, but when it's five in the morning, I only have it in me to do one batch, so I make big breakfast cookies, dropped on to the baking sheet in heaping tablespoons.

And sometimes I make a cherry almond version: instead of the walnuts and chocolate chips, add ½ cup slivered almonds and ¼ cup dried cherries; instead of vanilla, add almond extract.

Ingredients

    3 large ripe bananas, well mashed (about 1½ cups)
    ¼ cup coconut oil, warmed just a little so it isn't solid
      (or alternatively, olive oil)
    1 teaspoon vanilla
    2 cups rolled oats
    ⅔ cup almond meal

½ teaspoon sea salt
1 teaspoon baking powder
⅔ cup shredded coconut
½ cup chopped walnuts
¼ cup chocolate chips

Instructions

In a large bowl, mash the bananas with a fork, then add in coconut oil and vanilla.

Add the oats, almond meal, salt, and baking powder, and stir until combined. Add the coconut, walnuts, and chocolate chips, and stir again.

Form the dough into 12 balls on a parchment-lined baking sheet and flatten them a little bit. Bake at 350 degrees for 14 to 16 minutes.

MAKES: 12 cookies

morning, noon, and night

Winter turned to spring just when we were sure it never would. Springtime in Chicago is glorious—new life everywhere you look. And new life, gloriously, in our home too. I was thankful every day to be pregnant. Every morning, as soon as I was awake, I put my hands on my belly, almost to make sure it wasn't a dream. I talked to the baby all day long, whispering to it, urging it along: *Come on, baby; we can do this. We love you so much. Grow, baby. Please grow.*

My doctor assured me that the hemorrhage had diminished and the baby was safe. Unfortunately, there was nothing she could do about the fact that I had begun throwing up every day. Every day I thought I'd wake up feeling better, and every week someone would say, "You'll feel better by ten weeks." Or twelve weeks. Or sixteen weeks. But I threw up several times a day until the morning I delivered. I threw up like clockwork, three times every morning, usually once in the kitchen sink because I couldn't get to the bathroom fast enough. Then generally three more times throughout the day. The term "morning sickness" was not accurate. More accurate: "morning, noon, and night" sickness.

I tried all the different medicines they recommended, but they made no difference. I tried ginger in every form—capsules, chews, crystallized, ale. I ate saltines and dry toast some days, and other days, huge wedges of cantaloupe and icy-cold Coke. I ate sweet potato fries like they were going out of style. One week the only thing that sounded good was red Gatorade and red licorice. It didn't make any difference, though. I threw up every day, no matter what I ate, no matter what I did. I threw up in my car, off balconies, on planes. I threw up at playgrounds and on boats and at a wedding where I was a bridesmaid, almost eight months pregnant. I threw up while swimming, while in the shower, in the middle of the night, stumbling to the bathroom out of a dead sleep.

I tried to write from my bed, like a Victorian, but I wasn't getting a thing done. Not a thing. It's as though every creative cell in my body had been repurposed to vomiting. One thing that sometimes helped the vomiting was sleep, so lots of days when Aaron took Henry to school, I slept and read novels for most of the day.

I tried to keep speaking at the events I had scheduled throughout the spring, but after a hard trip during which I threw up into my own hand while I was driving on the interstate, my family staged an intervention: *no more traveling*. For the rest of the spring, summer, and early fall, my life was primarily about managing sickness, and everything else was a very distant second.

When it began, being sick was physical. After a while, though, being sick was also very, very emotional. Being sick forced me to confront the part of me that believes people only love me and keep me around because of what I can do for them. Some people are included because they're beautiful, or rich, or really smart. Some people are included because they're professionally successful. I get to stick around because I get stuff done. That's my thing. I'm a get-stuff-done person. I'm a utility player, a workhorse. And all of a sudden, I couldn't play. I couldn't work. I couldn't earn my keep, on practical and metaphysical levels. What would happen to me if I could no longer get things done?

I hated this person I had become, this person who couldn't be or do any of the things I wanted to be or do. The more I did, the sicker I was. And so I didn't do anything, and I ended up isolated and lonely, longing for the person I used to be—a person who lived her life with energy and excitement instead of the answer to everything being no. All the time: *no.*

My mind and heart were so full of intentions and desires and dreams—I wanted to plant herbs, go for walks, sort baby clothes. I wanted to take Henry to the farmers market, push him on the swings, teach him to ride a bike—all kinds of special things he and I could do before the baby came, special memories we'd have forever.

But instead the mom he saw was permanently somewhere between the couch and the bathroom. Every time he saw me run to the bathroom, he stood patiently outside the door and said, "Sorry you're barfing, Mom." Sweet boy.

I've long wanted to be better at accepting help, better at admitting weakness, better at trusting that people love me not for what I can do but just because they do. It would have been lovely to learn those things on my own terms, when I wanted to, the way I wanted to. But we never grow until the pain level gets high enough.

Being so sick for so long was a crash course, not one I would have chosen, not one I handled well, certainly. It was a painful education, but one I needed, one that forced me to embrace the risky but deeply beautiful belief that love isn't something you prove or earn, but something you receive or allow, like a balm, like a benediction, even when you're at your very worst.

Sweet Potato Fries with Sriracha Dipping Sauce

The love affair with sweet potato fries that began when I was pregnant has continued with much passion, so I set out to make baked sweet potato fries at home so we could indulge our cravings as often as we wanted. What this means, though, is that you can't expect super-crispy restaurant-style fries—that's only going to happen when there's deep-frying involved. What you can expect: yummy, light, flavorful sweet potato fries, and a dipping sauce that I think more than makes up for the lack of fried yumminess.

The thinner you slice the sweet potatoes, the crispier they'll be, and you really do have to line them up like soldiers, all in a row. If you pile them up on the pan willy-nilly, they'll clump up and steam and never get crispy.

Ingredients

    4 sweet potatoes
    ¼ cup olive oil, plus more for oiling pans
       Sea salt

Dipping sauce:
    ½ cup mayonnaise
    ½ cup ketchup
    1 teaspoon Sriracha sauce

Instructions

Preheat the oven to 425 degrees and put two rimmed baking sheets in the oven to warm up.

Peel and slice the sweet potatoes into long, thin batons—the thinner, the better. Pull the hot pans out of the oven and oil them, being careful not to burn yourself.

Toss the sweet potatoes with olive oil, then line them up on the baking sheets so they're not touching or overlapping.

Put both pans into the oven and bake for 10 minutes. After 10 minutes, switch the pans and give them a shake while you're at it, turning the batons.

Bake for another 6 to 10 minutes, depending on how crispy you'd like them. Remove when they start to become golden, but don't expect them to be completely crispy like deep-fried french fries — if you do, you'll overcook them.

Sprinkle with sea salt before serving.

While the sweet potato batons are cooking, mix together the mayonnaise, ketchup, and Sriracha in a small bowl. Serve alongside warm fries.

SERVES: 4

what my mother
taught me

One of the most important things my mom taught me—or, really, is teaching me over and over even now—is that the best is yet to come.

Everyone knows those kids who peak in middle school. Or high school. Or college. My mom is sixty, and she's never been cooler. My mom is a global soul: a poet, an activist, a woman of creativity and conviction and vision, a woman I aspire to be like in a million ways.

Over the years, my mom has been a social worker, a flutist, a stay-at-home mom, a writer, an editor, an oil painter, a potter, a world traveler, a contemplative, and a volunteer global ministry leader. She's an avid reader, an involved and loving grandma, a leading expert in the American Christian community on peacemaking in the Middle East. In the last few years, she's been to the Congo and the Middle East several times each. She loves to arrange flowers, and she loves to travel to the darkest places on earth and bring their stories back home to us.

When I get frustrated that there aren't enough hours in a day, that I can't do enough or be enough or experience everything I want to just exactly right now, my mom reminds me in her gentle way that this is not where she thought she'd be at sixty, and that the best is yet to come.

She teaches me, through her words and her actions, that if you take the next right step, if you live a life of radical and honest prayer, if you allow yourself to be led by God's Spirit, no matter how far from home and familiarity it takes you, you won't have to worry about what you want to be when you grow up. You'll be too busy living a life of passion and daring.

My mom turned sixty last November. My best friends and hers gathered around my dinner table for lots of food and wine and laughter and storytelling. I've known her best friends for years, of course, but as the night went on, I realized I didn't know how they all came to be friends. One after another, these women I've known for decades told the stories of how they first became connected with my mom. And the constant in all those stories is that her honesty invited them to be honest too. Her writing and speaking and truth telling—so deeply against the grain for most pastors' wives—made these women feel like they could tell the truth too. Some of them sought her out in the darkest seasons of their lives because she had written so honestly about the darkest seasons of her own life.

We sat around that table for hours, my friends and hers, plates filled and refilled, glasses filled and refilled. We told stories and read poems and passages from the Bible and lines from songs, toasting and celebrating all the ways my mom has made our lives better, has inspired us and set us free, and has been an example for us of how life can be if we dare.

Sometimes I meet women who are so passionate they're about to jump out of their skin. Their kids are getting older and the house is quiet and they want to do something. They want to get their hands really dirty and dive neck deep into something that keeps them up at night. They don't know what to do. They don't know how to move forward, so they're vibrating with pent-up passion turning rapidly to frustration.

And when I talk to them, I tell them the story of my mom. I tell them there's still so much time and still so much to be done. I tell them it doesn't have to be full-time, or all-or-nothing, or all-at-once. I tell them what my mom tells me — that you just have to take one step, and that when you do, the next one will appear. I tell them the path doesn't have to be a straight line, and that often it only makes sense when you look back at it. I tell them that when my mom was my age, she was a stay-at-home mom. She wasn't yet an oil painter or a potter or an AIDS activist or an expert on peacekeeping. There's still time, I tell them and I tell myself. *There's still time.*

My mom makes sixty look good, and she reminds me every day that honest prayers transform us, that the world is big and beautiful and waiting for us, and that the best *is* yet to come.

Real Simple Cassoulet

Adapted from Real Simple *magazine.*

Everything about this recipe is vintage Mom — it's healthful and simple and flavorful, but stylish and a bit unusual. It's a twist on a classic, familiar but new. She's made it a thousand times, and now I make it too. Most recently, we made this dish for our Easter meal up at the lake. As I've mentioned, pastors' families tend to run on different calendars because our holidays tend to center around church gatherings.

After all the Good Friday services and Easter services, we're sort of festived-out, and the last thing we want to do is sit around a fussy, formal table eating ham and lamb cake and jelly beans. There's nothing wrong with that, of course, but after lots of services and people and holiday merriment, all we want is to get to the lake.

We change into fleeces and boots; we drag the Adirondack chairs to the edge of the bluff; we let the boys run and run and run. After the sun sets on the water and the chill in the air finally drives us inside, we gather around the table, most often for something like cassoulet and Green Well Salad, warm and homey, unfussy and flavorful.

This is not a traditional cassoulet—are you sensing a theme? We use turkey sausage, olive oil, and bread crumbs made from gluten-free brown rice bread toasted and then whizzed up in the food processor. That makes it suitable for most dietary restrictions—dairy-free, gluten-free, OK for non-red-meat eaters.

I've served this cassoulet for dinner parties and for both casual and formal gatherings, and it never fails. It surprises people with flavor and warmth and nuance—it's the parsnips, I think. They're the secret weapon.

Ingredients

- 1 tablespoon olive oil
- 1 pound turkey Italian sausage, casings removed
- 1½ cups chicken broth
- 1 onion, thinly sliced
- 3 carrots, diced
- 3 parsnips, diced
- 1 tomato, chopped, or one 8-ounce can whole tomatoes, drained and chopped
- 3 15-ounce cans cannellini beans, drained
- 5 sprigs fresh thyme or 1 teaspoon dried thyme
- ½ teaspoon salt
- ⅛ teaspoon pepper
- 3 cloves garlic, minced
- 1 cup bread crumbs (we use gluten-free bread)
- ¼ cup fresh parsley, chopped
- 2 tablespoons butter, melted (or olive oil, for dairy-free eaters)

Instructions

In a skillet or frying pan, heat the oil over medium heat. Cook the sausage until well browned, breaking it up with a wooden spoon. Remove and drain on paper towels; set aside.

In a stock pot or dutch oven over medium-low heat, combine the chicken broth, vegetables, beans, thyme, salt, pepper, one-third of the garlic, and the sausage. Bring to a boil.

Reduce heat to low, cover, and simmer, stirring occasionally for about 1 hour, until thickened and the vegetables are tender.

Heat oven to 400 degrees. Pour cassoulet into an ovenproof dish. In a bowl, combine the bread crumbs, parsley, butter, and remaining garlic. Sprinkle evenly over the cassoulet, and place in the oven. Bake, uncovered, until the crust is golden brown, 10 to 15 minutes.

To make ahead and freeze, prepare without the bread crumb topping. Cover and freeze up to 4 months. When ready to cook, uncover the cassoulet, sprinkle with the bread crumb mixture, and bake, unthawed, 45 minutes to 1 hour at 400 degrees.

SERVES: 6

cupcake in the oven

I'm a big fan of breaking the rules, so for Blaine and Margaret's
baby shower, we bypassed the traditional route—ladies, fruit
salad, passing around little outfits—in favor of a Friday night
dinner party for couples. Blaine was possibly the most excited and
involved dad-to-be I'd ever seen, and to keep him from a shower
seemed cruel and unusual. Margaret is an expert baker, and both
Blaine and Margaret are paper-and-design people, so our friend
Lindsay made the most extraordinary invitations and menu cards
—palest pink and charcoal gray, with clean, modern little cupcakes
on everything.

Kristi had offered their home for the shower—I was pregnant
and sick, and Kristi's kitchen is pretty much my idea of heaven. The
first time I went to Kristi's house for a party, a mutual friend said,
"I had just been feeling so content and thankful for my house. Now
I want to burn it to the ground and move in here forever."

It's that kind of house, where you want to move in forever
—stylish and beautiful, all grays and silvers and whites, classic
and modern at the same time. When Kristi invited us to throw the
shower there, I couldn't say yes fast enough.

We dreamed up a make-your-own grilled cheese bar, with
tomato bisque, Caesar salad, and cupcakes: fresh strawberry and
salted caramel and chocolate. The plan was for the Cooking Club
to come to Kristi's on Friday afternoon to prep and cook together.

On that Friday morning, though, I got an email from Kristi. The first line read, *I'm writing this because I can't say it out loud.*

Her healthy, active mom had gone to the ER the night before and come home with a diagnosis of advanced liver cancer. Kristi was seven months pregnant with their first child, but they got permission from their doctor to leave that night to be with her mother in Calgary—two flights and many hours away.

I read and reread the email, and then I put my head down on the steering wheel and sobbed in my car, feeling scared for Kristi and for her mom. I raced home, and Aaron had just received a similar email from Kristi's husband, Matt. I started throwing things in a bag—Lärabars, magazines, a book I thought might be good company on the flight, chocolates, mixed nuts.

I didn't know Kristi very well at that point. We'd had a few long, rambling conversations on my couch or hers while our husbands were at rehearsals together. We'd been to their house in Cape Cod the summer before, but what we didn't have were those galvanizing experiences that long-term friendships carry, so I didn't really know what to do in that moment. I knew, though, that in my own moments of greatest loss, I told people I was fine, and then when they saw through my attempt to be strong and alone, I was so incredibly grateful.

So I sent Kristi a text: *I'm on my way with a few things for the plane. If you want me to come in, let me know, and if I don't hear from you, I'll just leave a bag on your back porch.*

As I drove, I called Margaret and the other Cooking Club girls. Kristi wrote in her email that they wanted us to continue without them and would leave the house ready for the party. But when I put myself in her place, I thought the last thing she needed was the pressure to leave the house perfect for entertaining. She should be able to throw things on the floor while she was packing, leave a mess, focus on getting out the door and not on getting the house party-ready.

Kristi texted back that she did want me to come in, and we hugged and cried and she gave me an update. And then she said she was all set to host the shower. I told her we'd host, of course, that I didn't want her to have to do one more thing.

You didn't tell them to move houses, did you? I told you. I want to do this. She became something between stern and panicked, her light eyes turning steely.

I didn't know what to do. I wanted to help her. I wanted to make things easier, and I know that sometimes in those kinds of moments I need someone to help me pry my hands off something. We just stared at each other for a moment, and right then, her husband, Matt, called and Kristi put him on the speaker. *Matt, Shauna's trying to move the party. Tell her not to do that. Tell her we really want to have it here.*

Matt, always the peacemaker, always the lightener of moods, said, *Oh, Shauna, now's not the time to cross our girl. I wouldn't do that if I were you.*

Kristi's eyes filled with tears. She was almost pleading. *It's all done. We're ready. I need to know that something will stay the way it was.*

And then I understood. What *I* may have needed or not needed in that moment didn't matter a bit. What my friend Kristi needed was totally different. She needed to know that something was going as planned while everything else felt so deeply out of control. And I would do anything she wanted in order to help her in that moment.

And so we did. I came back a few hours later, and Kristi's stylish, last-minute touches were all over the house—flowers on the island, hand towels in the guest bathroom, a sweet note for Blaine and Margaret on the counter.

It was a miserable March evening—a dark sky and a sleeting rain, the kind that chills you till your teeth rattle. The Cooking Club arrived at Kristi's house one by one, bearing cheese and fruit and soup. We worked alongside one another, mostly in silence, slicing apples, scooping mustards and tapenades into ramekins, frosting cupcakes.

And when all the guests arrived, before we blessed the food, we told them the little we knew about Kristi's mom, and in a circle in that kitchen, we prayed together—for Kristi's mom, for Matt and Kristi as they traveled, for their baby. We prayed as well for Blaine and Margaret's baby, the one we had gathered to celebrate. The rain fell in icy sheets, hitting the kitchen windows with a harsh cracking sound, like someone was throwing handfuls of fine gravel at them over and over.

Inside the house, we were warm, and the kitchen was filled with an almost palpable sense of prayer and connectedness. We were celebrating and mourning; we were praying for help and peace and health. Being in Matt and Kristi's home made us feel connected to them, even in their absence, and every time I ran my hand over the surface of the counter, or wiped a glass and put it back in a cabinet, I prayed for them.

Melody's tomato bisque was rich and creamy, the perfect antidote to the weather, and Brannon's Caesar is an all-time favorite, just a touch spicy and quite lemony. We laid out platters and plates of all different cheeses and breads—gouda, cheddar, goat cheese, baguette, whole grain, sourdough. And meats and fruits and mustards and tapenades. People piled up sandwiches, and we helped them navigate the panini presses. Some were adventurous, and some were traditionalists, but as the night went on, we shared our favorites—try salami with fontina! Here, try an apple slice with the gouda!

We oohed and aahed over the baby clothes; we chatted and

ate soup and cupcakes. And even though the weather was awful, or maybe because it was, we stayed for ages, leaning against counters, snuggling into the corners of couches.

I think we needed, in literal and figurative ways, a harbor in the tempest, a port in the storm. We felt connected to Blaine and Margaret and the sacred and amazing ways that a new baby would transform their lives. And we felt connected to Matt and Kristi too, sitting around their table while they flew across the continent, full of fear and anguish. We didn't want to leave, and so we didn't, for hours and hours.

After that day, Kristi and I laughed about that moment, standing in her kitchen, two tough women, each one trying to persuade the other. I apologized for trying to give her what *I* would have needed, not what she needed. And when I think about my friendship with her, I don't think about the easy moments—the gifts she's given me, the times we've laughed or gone out to lunch. I think about that email, that moment in her kitchen, when she allowed me into the most fragile place in her life, when I clumsily tried to help and only made it worse, and when I finally understood what would help her most.

That was a year ago. Kristi's daughter, Elsa, and Margaret's daughter, Ruby, were both born safe and healthy. Kristi's mom is beating the odds every day, after a radical surgery this summer. The pictures of her holding Elsa make me weep with gratitude because I remember the unspoken fear as they packed for their visit—that Kristi's mom would not meet their daughter. The grace and goodness of seeing her with her granddaughter silence me.

We don't learn to love each other well in the easy moments. Anyone is good company at a cocktail party. But love is born when we misunderstand one another and make it right, when we cry in the kitchen, when we show up uninvited with magazines and granola bars, in an effort to say, *I love you.*

feasting and fasting

A few summers ago, after a season of vacation and celebration, I began a fast. It's a diet, for lack of a better term—limiting my food intake to only lean proteins, fruits, and vegetables, with just a few whole grains. No dairy, caffeine, or alcohol. No gluten or sugar. Loads of water, piles of greens. There should be a better term than *diet*, because *diet* conjures up sugar-free Jell-O and deprivation, aspartame and fake food, and years and years of shame and misguided discipline.

The word that helps me these days is *fasting*, although I'll plead permission to use it loosely. I have fasted strictly, as a spiritual discipline, consuming only broth and juice for a certain amount of time. But I'm using the word *fasting* these days as an opposite term to *feasting*—yin and yang, up and down, permission and discipline, necessary slides back and forth along the continuum of how we feed ourselves.

Maybe certain people can develop a food perspective that they maintain seamlessly twelve months a year. Good for them. Maybe that's something I'll be able to do when I'm all grown-up and filled with moderation and wisdom. Probably not, though. I think I just might be one of those people who will always need some guardrails along the way.

I love the feasting part of life. I don't want Thanksgiving without stuffing or Christmas without cookies and champagne. I don't want to give up our family tradition of deep-frying everything we can think of on New Year's Eve. But I'm learning that feasting can only exist healthfully—physically, spiritually, and emotionally—in a life that also includes fasting.

The weeks between Thanksgiving and New Year's are, for me, a feast. Sage stuffing, sweet potato biscuits with maple butter. I love the traditions and tastes of the season—Aunt Mary's raisin bread, toasted and topped with melting sharp cheddar slices; my mother-in-law's apple-sized peanut butter truffles; my cousin's dark chocolate sea salted toffee.

For all those reasons and a thousand more, the holiday season isn't one I want to spend eating nothing but greens. I love being present to every bite of it, tasting it, absorbing every part of it. And then with January comes a time to fast, to recalibrate my appetites, both physically and emotionally. Fasting gives me a chance to practice the discipline of not having what I want at every moment, of limiting my consumption, making space in my body and in my spirit for a new year, one that's not driven by my mouth, by wanting, by consuming.

The other feasting season in my life is summer. We move up to the lake and pretend we own a bed-and-breakfast, a house full of friends and kids, an endless cycle of washing sheets and towels. It's no time for moderation. We take the kids to the beach and stop for pizza on the way home, balancing the boxes on our wagons full of sandy, happy, tired kids. We eat fresh blueberry pie for breakfast with strong, dark coffee, and gobble up steak tacos wrapped in tiny foil bundles from Su Casa. We stand in line at Sherman's Dairy, waiting for our number to be called, debating flavors—chocolate malt supreme? Coconut almond fudge? Blue moon?—just the way we did when we were little.

And then the summer ends, and we pack up all the towels and life jackets and sand toys. When we get home, the fast begins

—appropriate, timely, the right next step in the dance of feasting and fasting.

I'm a person of great appetites. I love to eat. I love to talk about food, think about food, play with food. The grocery store is my happy place, and the farmers market is my shrine. I'm never happier than when I'm planning a menu or passing bowls around my table, fragrant and full.

At the same time, though, every holiday season my jeans get too tight, and every summer I could swear that someone has shrunk my swimsuit bottoms. I so easily let my appetites get away from me—one more glass of red wine, one more slice of sharp cheddar cheese on raisin bread, one more forkful of vinegary, salty french potato salad every time I walk by it.

A few years ago, after a particularly indulgent summer, I went to a natural health doctor. Not just because of the weight I'd gained (again), but also because I had the sense that in all sorts of ways, my body wasn't working the way it should. I was getting sick more easily than usual. I still hadn't conceived, after months of trying. My neck and shoulders throbbed, the muscles brittle as bones. Chiropractic adjustments and massage weren't helping, and the amount of Advil I was taking to manage the pain seemed troubling. I woke up every night at 3:00 a.m., unable to get back to sleep, and I was nauseous most mornings, which felt especially cruel with each passing month I wasn't pregnant.

I was, in a word, desperate enough to do what I hadn't been willing to do before. I've seen many friends and family members, my husband included, benefit from cutting out this or that. Aaron would say that eating gluten-free has been a life-changing move for him.

But still. Really. Food is my thing. I don't smoke. I don't do drugs. I don't have a secret online shopping addiction. But I eat. I love to eat. And in my very honest moments, I have to admit that giving up food and wine felt like more than I could manage. What I eat and what I drink are little moments of joy throughout the day—the things I think about, plan around, daydream about. I love the moment when I open the menu at a restaurant or start prepping to make dinner or uncork the wine. On long writing days, those breaks for bread and cheese or leftover cold pasta or a slice of Emily's poppy seed cake dipped into espresso are the little motivators that keep me writing.

But if the last few years have taught me anything at all, it's that the very things you think you need most desperately are the things that can transform you the most profoundly when you do finally decide to release them. The college I had my heart set on, the boyfriend I believed would be my husband, the job that defined me, the pregnancy I believed would end a season of longing and loss. Each one, pulled from my grubby fists, each one teaching me something fundamental about desire and transformation. Over and over, I learn the hard way that the thing I'm clinging to can be the thing that sets me free.

So I called the doctor, and on a warm summer night, he broke the news: no gluten, no dairy, no caffeine, no alcohol, no sugar. Didn't he know that my favorite food groups are bread, cheese, wine, and coffee? But against all odds, I was ready. No one changes their life until the pain level is unmanageable, and in all sorts of ways for me, the pain level had reached the unmanageable point. I followed his advice for more than four months. I felt great. I lost some weight, started sleeping better, didn't ache at all. Success!

But at the same time, I felt like I wasn't living in the same world everyone else was living in. It was like choosing to live with the volume turned all the way down, or going to the beach but not being able to put my feet in the ocean. My senses were starving. Eating such a restricted diet on an ongoing basis wasn't going to work for me. It worked through the fall, but began to fall apart in advance of Christmas, predictably, and unraveled completely on vacation—conch fritters, rum punch. To not eat and drink those things that were so connected to that place I'd come to love over the years felt counter to the way I wanted to live. There has to be a way to live with health and maturity and intention while still honoring the part of me that loves to eat, that sees food as a way to nurture and nourish both my body and my spirit.

I'm working to find a middle ground—some fasting, some feasting. At some points, gobbling up life with every bite; in other seasons, mastering the appetites and tempering the desires. My work these days is to find that fine balance—allowing my senses to taste every bite of life without being driven by appetites, indiscriminate and ravenous. Some days I get it right, and some days I don't, but I do know that along the way, the process is healing me.

Robin's Super-Healthy Lentil Soup

When I've been doing a little too much feasting and need to bring things back a little bit, this is my go-to. I make a big pot of my friend Robin's lentil soup, sometimes doubling the recipe. It's so helpful for me to have something healthful and flavorful and—most important—already prepared. This is an endlessly versatile recipe, as most of my favorite recipes are. Sometimes I add leeks or shallots instead of garlic and onions, and I love adding fresh rosemary or a little rosemary salt at the end with the vinegar. A dusting of Parmesan dresses it up for guests, as does some fresh parsley or celery leaves.

Ingredients
   3 tablespoons extra-virgin olive oil
   2 cups onions, chopped

 1 cup celery stalks, chopped
 1 cup carrots, chopped
 2 garlic cloves, chopped
 6 cups chicken or vegetable broth
1½ cups lentils
 1 14.5-ounce can diced tomatoes in juice
    Balsamic vinegar
    Salt and pepper to taste

Instructions

Heat oil in heavy large saucepan over medium-high heat.

Add onions, celery, carrots, and garlic; sauté until vegetables begin to brown, about 15 minutes.

Add broth, lentils, and tomatoes with juice, and bring to boil.

Reduce heat to medium-low, cover, and simmer until lentils are tender, about 35 minutes.

Season with salt, pepper, and a splash of vinegar.

SERVES: 6

love and enchiladas

One of the best parts about our six years in Grand Rapids was this little band of friends we made, something like a tribe, very much like a family. We laughed and cried and shared lawn care equipment. We visited each other in the hospital when our babies were born. We grilled out and spent weekends at the lake and up north, and we gathered around the table what seems like a million times.

If you've been part of a church, you know there are practically a hundred names for "a little group of people who meet regularly to learn and pray and walk through life." They're called small groups or community groups or life groups or whatever. For about ten seconds at our church in Grand Rapids, these gatherings were called house churches, and it happened to be during that exact ten-second period that we formed our little group. So that's what we called it. At some point, someone—probably Annette, because she's prone to nicknaming—referred to the group as The Hidey Hole, but that's so creepy that we stuck with house church, even though it's not particularly accurate. House church conjures up secret meetings in basements in China, not dinner every Wednesday in Grand Rapids, but it stuck, and now it seems we're the HC forever.

When we all lived in Grand Rapids, we had dinner together once a week, and after dinner we'd move to the living room to talk and pray. Once our babies were born—first Spence, then Henry, then Emerson—we'd take a break to put them to bed after dinner. I can assemble a Pack 'n Play in about ten seconds flat as a result of all those nights, baby on one hip, other arm clicking the rails into place and wrestling with the little sheet, shushing and patting, backing out of the room, trying not to make a sound.

They were our people, our stand-in family, our truth tellers, our problem solvers, our middle of the night phone calls and unannounced stopovers. Joe lived on the same street as Annette and Andrew, and they were all only two blocks from us. Steve and Sarah lived "far away," meaning you had to get in the car to get to their house, for about five whole minutes.

And then in the course of one year, it all shifted, and life scattered us. First Joe left on a sailing trip with my brother. Then a few months later, Annette and Andrew moved back to California. A year later, Joe moved back to Grand Rapids just before Steve and Sarah moved to Orange County, and we moved back to Chicago.

On the day the movers came to our house, Joe stopped by, and we walked through the empty rooms together. He'd been in those rooms as much as anyone, making dinner and playing poker and watching movies. We walked through them mostly in silence, trying to think of something to say that wasn't as terribly sad as what we were all feeling.

We knew when we moved away that something like this wouldn't necessarily happen again. It was a moment in time, a gift, an event that we happened to be a part of just for that season.

We gathered again for Joe and Emily's wedding. We all came into town a few days early and spent New Year's Eve together at Annette's family's cabin. We ate enchiladas and opened Christmas presents and danced around the living room, drinking margaritas and hugging and kissing at midnight. The next morning we made breakfast together, frying bacon, drinking coffee, cozy and sleepy.

The next year we all met in Santa Barbara. It rained the whole time, and Annette and Andrew were in the middle of moving houses, tired and overwhelmed by details. Steve was launching a new campus at their church, mind racing with plans and scenarios. Aaron was jet-lagged and shell-shocked, just back from his first trip to Israel and Palestine. I found out I was pregnant while we were there, which explained why I threw up outside a restaurant on State Street one night. The next month, I'd miscarry twins, but we didn't know that yet. My grandmother was dying, and I was on the phone with my dad a lot, every call nearer to the end.

It was a hard trip, for all those reasons and more, but one night we had dinner at The Palace—steaks and shrimp and their famous bread pudding soufflé with whiskey cream sauce. Like they always do, at ten o'clock the cooks and servers and hosts made sure everyone had a glass to raise, and the whole restaurant sang along with Louis Armstrong's gravelly version of "What a Wonderful World," swaying and clinking glasses. I've loved that restaurant and that tradition since my college days.

When I think back to that trip, it's gray and rainy, lots of awkward silences and painful phone calls and tired eyes, all of us trying to connect, but mostly missing. But I also think of that night, protected from the rain, singing and laughing. In the midst of it all, what a wonderful world indeed.

The next summer, we all came back to South Haven. Three of us were pregnant, and vacationing with pregnant people is sort of a recipe for disaster. But when they left, I cried hard, choking tears, bent over the sink. My heart ached as they left, because that thing, the thing we have when we're together, the thing we thought we left behind all those years ago, was alive and well, and it seemed cruel and unusual that we have to fly across the country to experience it.

This spring, our little family went to stay with Annette and

Andrew. One night, Annette made carne asada and guacamole. After the kids were in bed, the four of us picked up toys, chatting idly. At one point it turned to a conversation about me, about my life and my deepest and most unhealed self. It was honest and terrifying, and I kept saying, "I want to throw myself in the pool right now! This is truly horrible!" But they kept asking kind but hard questions and kept being their lovely, attentive, wise selves. I felt like I was at therapy times a thousand, and they just kept applying gentle pressure, being honest and letting me be ragged and strange.

The next morning, when we were drinking coffee and getting ready for church, I said, "You know, I had this terrible dream that instead of just chatting and having fun, we all had a super-serious, super-long conversation about, like, my whole entire life and identity. Isn't that a nightmare?" They smiled and laughed and told me that that's what friendship does. I know it does, but this was next-level—friendship times friendship times friendship.

We knew that the Grand Rapids season was singular, never to be repeated. But I don't think we knew the life and force and influence these friendships would have beyond that season. I don't think we knew that when we see each other a few times a year, there would still be that trust and honesty and love, that we would still care about each other in so many ways and understand each other so well, even across the distance and the times zones and the life changes.

There is so much, after all these years, that holds us together —honesty and inside jokes and hours logged and memories made and probably a thousand meals shared around the table. I remember french toast strata for one Easter, and lots of pizza on the boat in South Haven. I remember eating still-warm chocolate-chip cookies from Tom's Mom's Cookies in Harbor Springs and drinking piña coladas on Peter Island.

But more than anything, what we eat when we're together is Mexican food. Annette and Andrew are Californians, and Steve and Sarah nearly so. Joe is a guacamole aficionado of some repute, and since his birthday is the day before Cinco de Mayo, his birthday celebrations are always fiestas—margaritas, tacos and salsas, wedges of lime and sprinkles of cilantro, black beans and warm tortillas.

We've been eating Annette's enchiladas together for almost a decade. We've had them around her table dozens of times, and around mine, because her recipe is the only one I use—by far my favorite. We've had them in Santa Barbara on a rainy long weekend when none of us were at our best, and on a lovely, cozy New Year's Eve in Saugatuck just before Joe and Emily's wedding. When I think of the house church—whatever we call it or should have called it—I think of love, and I think of enchiladas.

Annette's Enchiladas

This is serious comfort food—like, "eat it with a fork straight out of the pan in the middle of the night" comfort food. When I served this to my friend Jorie for the first time, she described it as a chicken pot pie with green chilies, and that's a great way to put it.

These enchiladas are my go-to "new baby" meal. I'm not going to tell you this dish is particularly healthy, with all the sour cream and cheese. But here's the thing: when I was pregnant, I swore up and down that the second each of my babies was born, all I would want is fruit and lean meats. Possibly a veggie.

And with each child, I have distinct memories of destroying a pan of enchiladas late at night, standing in the kitchen alone. That may be just me, of course, and I'm not going to tell you that the only time I've done that is immediately postpartum, but what I am telling you is that no matter what the new mom says, I'm pretty sure she wants a pan of Annette's enchiladas.

You can adjust the level of heat by choosing mild or medium enchilada sauce and mild or medium chilies. For new moms, I use the mild version of both, but for anyone else, I do medium—the sour cream and cheese cut the heat a little bit.

You'll notice that these enchiladas aren't rolled but rather layered, more like a lasagna—it's all part of the awesome that is this recipe. The first reason this is sheer genius: you don't run into the problem of having the chicken get all dry and lonely rolled up inside the tortilla while all the good stuff is hanging out separately. Second, you don't have to portion it according to each rolled tortilla—this way, you just scoop out portions the way you would with lasagna.

When I'm taking this dish to a new mom, I add chips and salsa, black beans, and vanilla ice cream with caramel sauce. For Christmas one year, I gave my brother basically the same thing and called it "Dinner Party in a Box." I made a pan of enchiladas, and added chips, salsa, black beans, beer, and a jar of caramel sauce. In the card I added cooking instructions and told him to buy a lime, vanilla ice cream, and cilantro just before the party. He reported back to me that the beer, chips, and salsa were put to good use right away, and that the enchiladas were delicious, even after being in his freezer—for a year and a half.

Ingredients

- 1 cup sour cream
- 1 28-ounce can green enchilada sauce (Las Palmas is best)
- 2 4-ounce small cans green chilies, diced
- 3 cups cooked chicken, shredded or diced
- 2 cups Monterey Jack cheese, shredded
- 12 corn tortillas
- 1 cup chicken broth
- Cilantro

Instructions

Mix green sauce with chilies and sour cream.

Smooth 1 spoonful of the sauce mixture around the bottom of a 9 by 13 pan.

Simmer the chicken broth in a skillet, and before placing each tortilla in the 9 by 13 pan, use tongs to pass the tortilla through the broth for just a few seconds. If you leave the tortillas in the broth for too long, they'll fall apart, so just dip each one in for a few seconds to soften it before putting it in the enchilada pan.

Layer 4 tortillas over the first layer of sauce.

After tortillas, add half the chicken, then one-third of the sauce, then one-third of the cheese.

Repeat so there are 2 full layers.

Finish with a layer of 4 more tortillas, the remaining third of the sauce, and the remaining third of the cheese.

Bake at 350 degrees until warmed through and the cheese is melted, about 30 to 35 minutes.

Let sit at least 15 minutes before cutting. Top with chopped cilantro.

SERVES: 6

meeting mac

Last year we spent Easter at the lake with my family, heading over after the holiday services at church were finished. It was cold, but we took the boat out anyway, bundled up and huddled together, noses red and cheeks cold to the touch. We thawed out at the cottage later, with hot chocolate and a fire in the fireplace. The next morning, we had a big breakfast and then a lazy morning in front of the fire. In the afternoon, Aaron left for a concert in the city, but I was too sick for a concert, so Henry and I stayed at the lake a little longer with my family.

Just after I kissed Aaron good-bye, I got a call from my doctor. I was eighteen weeks along, and when I saw the doctor's office phone number on the caller ID, I assumed the office manager was confirming an upcoming appointment. But it was my doctor's voice on the line, and she called me sweetie. And then I knew something horrible was coming.

My test results were in, tests I barely remembered having undergone. She was so sorry, but we needed to see a specialist. She was so sorry, but the test results suggested a serious chromosomal abnormality, many versions of which would mean the baby wouldn't survive the pregnancy.

The information was coming so fast that I couldn't make it make sense. I was nodding, as though she could see me, and as the information and the numbers blurred together in my mind, I covered my mouth and began to sob. I was looking out at the lake, still and steely gray.

My parents were playing with Henry on the hammock, and I could hear them laughing. My dad came up to the house, and his face rearranged completely when he saw my tears. Henry's construction paper and markers were all over the coffee table, and I wrote the word DOCTOR in red marker on white paper, and then began scribbling as many numbers and words and statistics as I could get down. He sat next to me and tried to make sense of my scribbles as I kept nodding along with the doctor's voice.

This was the first thing my dad said after I hung up the phone: "This child will be so loved. No matter what. This family has so much love to give. *No matter what.* We love this child already." I kept that piece of construction paper—stained with my tears, scribbled with terrible words, folded up in my wallet—for months.

Aaron and I went to the specialist the next week, and he gave us numbers upon numbers. Rates, statistics, percentages. Every time we asked him a question—a question we wanted answered with words, ideas, stories—he answered instead with more numbers. It was like talking to a very kind calculator, but it didn't help us understand.

What we realized, essentially, is that we wouldn't know until delivery if there was, in fact, a chromosomal abnormality and what that meant for the baby. We had just enough information to make us crazy and scared, and not nearly enough to know anything of substance. It felt like a nightmare that began again every time we closed our eyes—fear and tears and anxiety, but nothing real, nothing to know or to stand on.

And so we waited. Miserably. We prayed. Sometimes we prayed for the baby to be perfectly healthy. And sometimes we prayed for God's will to be done, and that we would be the best parents to this child, whatever challenges he faced. When we prayed for a healthy baby, we didn't even really know what that meant. Healthier than what?

It felt like a sucker punch. All the waiting, then the joy, then the hemorrhage, then the all clear, then the sickness. To cheer me up, people kept saying, "It will all be worth it when you're holding a healthy baby." But what if there would be no healthy baby? What if there would be no baby? What if the hardest, most painful season was still to come?

Under the sickness, I harbored the test results like a tumor, like a land mine buried just under the surface. I could feel it there all the time. We didn't tell anyone but our parents and two very close friends, because saying it made it more real than we could handle. I tried not to flinch when people told me over and over that the sickness would all be worth it when I held my healthy baby. I tried not to betray my secret. I tried to pray—to put this baby in God's hands every day, over and over—but on some days all I wanted in the world was to know the future, even if it was terrible. I wanted to peer into my own belly like looking into an aquarium or a crystal ball. What's happening in there? Who are you, baby? Will we know you, hold you, raise you?

The days were excruciatingly long, and I felt my own anxiety ratcheting up as my due date neared. Every good appointment gave me hope, but the numbers screamed in my head.

And then. And then. And then our boy, our healthy boy, was born. We drove to the hospital in the dark, early on a Monday morning, the ER empty and silent. My labor was fast and hard, and the epidural didn't have time to take effect. The nurse yelled for the doctor. "Now! We need you now!"—and she came running in, pulling on her gloves. Aaron and my mom and my mother-in-law took turns holding my hands, and I cried out like my bones were breaking, and less than five hours after we arrived at the hospital, our baby boy was born—healthy and strong.

I asked the pediatrician over and over again, "Is he all right? What's going on? He's all right?" He didn't know what I meant until I told him about our test results and our odds, and after listening to me, he dismissed my question out of hand. "This baby is as healthy as can be," he said emphatically. He said it again: "You have a completely healthy baby boy."

Those words sounded like music, like magic.

While the nurses bathed our baby and measured him, our dads joined us, peering over the nurses' shoulders to see him. While my dad held William MacIntyre, his namesake, for the first time, Aaron's dad said a prayer, and his voice was low and clear and steady as he thanked God for Mac's healthy birth. Our miracle, our baby Mac.

part three

God never meant man to be a purely spiritual creature. That is why He uses material things like bread and wine to put the new life into us. We may think this rather crude and unspiritual. God does not: He invented eating. He likes matter. He invented it.

C. S. LEWIS, *Mere Christianity*

hail mary

Right from the beginning, Mac was a dream—a snuggler, an easy sleeper, a good eater. We had almost twenty visitors at the hospital that first day, and ten the next. Our parents were there most of the day, and then Aaron's sister brought Henry and his cousin. The Cooking Club came, and they filled the room with baby blankets and outfits, homemade cookies and honeycrisp apples. They wanted to hear every detail while they crowded around the bed. My brother drove out from the city at the end of the day with a fancy bottle of champagne. After the noise and chaos of so many guests had faded, he held Mac for a long time in our silent room, late into the night.

After we came home from the hospital, my mother-in-law and my mom were over all the time, and my dad's car seemed to drive itself over to our house every day after work. The weather was still warm, the afternoon sun golden and sparkling through the trees, and we went for lots of walks as the shadows extended across the sidewalk.

Our friends and family kept our house full of apples and soup, salad and enchiladas and pumpkin bread. They brought Mac sleepers and blankets, and dropped off gallons of cider and cookies. The Cooking Club filled our freezer with shepherd's pie and beef bourguignon and spicy tomatillo chicken chili.

The days were a sweet blur of feedings and visits and naps in my arms, folding baby clothes and slicing honeycrisps for Henry. And then when he was ten days old, Mac seemed a little fussy. He wasn't sleeping as well, and he wanted to be held. He was ten days old, though, and I barely knew him, it seemed, or what was normal for him.

By evening, I was a little more concerned, and every time I took his temperature, it was completely different—over 101 one time, then 97 the next. I thought about swaddling and rocking him and putting him down in the crib. I'd be right there if he needed me since I was still sleeping in the nursery.

I called my neighbor Pam, and she told me to call the doctor. She told me I'd worry all night if I didn't, and she was right. I hung up the phone and called the doctor. I was fairly certain she'd tell me to give him a little Tylenol maybe, or take him to the office in the morning. But she told me to take him straight to the ER, and to expect blood and urine tests and a lumbar puncture—what used to be called a spinal tap.

She said she was telling me this on the phone so I didn't freak out when I got to the ER. I was sobbing before I even hung up. I kept saying to Aaron, "We were just watching *The Office*. I was about to put him to bed. I almost put him to bed."

When I hung up, there was a text from Pam offering to come over and stay with Henry. I realized she knew this drill so much better than I did, and before I even had the diaper bag packed, she was at my door—nothing short of an angel right when we needed one.

And then all of a sudden, our boy—our miracle, our ten-day-old son—was on a hospital bed with a team of doctors and nurses taking blood from his arms and his feet, catheterizing him, asking me to sign a form to authorize the lumbar puncture. His fever was much higher than we thought, and when I saw the number on the monitor, I cried out. I kept saying, "I almost didn't come. I almost went to bed."

I wish I could tell you that some mother instinct made me strong in that moment, that I was clearheaded and resolute, calm. Instead I wept out loud, trying to catch my breath, ragged and weak, terrified. At one point, the ER doctor stopped talking and reached over and tapped my knee with two fingers, just for a second. "Are we OK, Mom?" he asked. He told me that he and his wife, who is also a doctor, have three little boys, and that their baby had a high fever once. He told me he understood how scared I was.

They mentioned something in passing about moving him to his room, and I realized they were admitting him, admitting us. Their fear was that the fever was caused by spinal meningitis, and they had to begin treating him right away. After forty-eight hours, the tests would tell us more. I was entirely disoriented. We had just been in the hospital the week before for his birth. How could we be here again? We had just been watching *The Office*. I almost went to bed. I almost went to bed.

After we found out we were staying, we asked Aaron's mom to relieve Pam and stay with Henry. After all the tests were done, after Mac vomited all over my neck and down my shirt, after the IV needle was inserted and taped down on his tiny foot, after he was finally settled and nursing in my arms, Aaron got a call from his mother.

Henry had woken up crying hard, with a cough that sounded like a barking dog. He wasn't breathing well. Henry was scared, and my mother-in-law was worried. She wanted Aaron to come home. We didn't even talk about the improbability of this; we didn't even say anything like, "What are the chances?" He told his mom he'd be there soon, and I called my dad and asked him to come to the hospital. My mom was out of town, but clearly, my dad had just been waiting for the invitation, because he came into the ER about five minutes later, in a dress shirt and navy blazer.

He came in and hugged me and kissed Mac, and Aaron went home to Henry. The only moment of levity I remember from that night is that while we were still in the ER, waiting to be admitted to the PICU, my dad paced back and forth over and over in front of the pediatric ER desk in his blazer. I asked him at a certain point why he was pacing—and, incidentally, why he was so dressed up. Had he come from an event?

No, he said he'd been at home, but that he was dressed to intimidate and he was pacing to create some action. We all do strange things under stress: I cry like a faucet has been turned on, and my dad dresses to intimidate, and he paces.

By the time Aaron got home, Henry was doing a little better, and he planned to take him to the doctor in the morning. It didn't seem he needed to come to the ER.

They got us to our room by 2:00 a.m. Before my dad left, we sat across from one another in silence, both fixing our eyes on Mac, so tiny in one of those great big terrible pediatric cribs that look like cages, all bars and levers, medieval and cruel.

And then my dad left, and I was alone with Mac. I sat in a rocker next to the terrible crib, holding his tiny hand, too wrung out even to cry any more tears. The nurses and techs came in every hour to check his IV or to give him more medicine. In the silence, I realized I would miss Henry's fifth birthday, which was the next day. I had thought my tears were gone, but the prospect of missing Henry's birthday felt like tearing open a wound, and the tears began again.

One of my great working-mom regrets is that I missed Henry's fourth birthday. I was in the middle of a book tour, and I was asked to take part in a large event, not the kind, certainly, that could be moved for my schedule. Aaron and I talked about it. Aaron would be with him, and I left a wrapped present for every day I was gone,

one to open each day of his birthday week. I talked to him on the phone, and my mother-in-law made a special celebration day for him. But I was a wreck. I had done the wrong thing.

And so I had resolved to make Henry's fifth birthday special. I would be there, of course, and it would not get lost in the blur and excitement of a new baby. We had a party the week before Mac was born, well before Henry's actual birthday, because I was so determined not to miss it. Henry wore a little shirt with a "5" on it, and he ran around with friends and cousins, and I was so pregnant and tired and overwhelmed that at one point, I just went and sat in the car for a minute.

We had a special day planned for his actual birthday—presents and balloons first thing in the morning, lunch at his favorite restaurant, a whole day dedicated to making him feel special. And now I was in the hospital with the baby, and because Henry was sick, he couldn't come to visit, and because I couldn't leave the baby, I couldn't go home to be with him.

Looking back, I can see now that I shouldn't have been alone that night. Of course Aaron had to be home with Henry. Of course my dad needed to get home and get some sleep. My mom was furiously changing flights to get back home, but she wasn't home yet. I had sent my cousin and a few friends a text in the middle of the night that I figured they wouldn't get until morning—but my cousin saw it and offered to come to the hospital right then. I said no because she works full-time and has a little girl and a baby, and I couldn't do that to her, but looking back on it, I wish I had said yes, because there in that hospital in the cold, dark middle of the night, I felt as fragile and afraid as I had ever felt, like you could have sliced me open with a breath.

I was still recovering from the birth, still bleeding, still sore, still taking pain medication, and I had nothing there with me but a diaper bag and my phone. I was hungry and scared and angry.

I felt tricked. For so many months, things had been hard and scary. I had been so sick for so long, and we had worried so desperately for so long. And then things were fine. I was just getting used to things being fine. Our baby boy was born healthy. We had all made it through. And now this? What did this mean? Why were we back to fear again? What was happening to us?

It sounds crazy, maybe, or hyperbolic, but that night was possibly the bleakest of my life—I felt insubstantial to the point of transparency, like my bones and blood were gone and I was vapor, a ghost in a rocking chair. I felt profoundly, deeply alone. It was no one's fault, of course, or possibly only mine. I could have asked for company, and I know my friends and family would have come. But I was too far removed. I was on autopilot, and I didn't know what I needed, let alone how to say it.

Sleep was impossible, because someone was in the room every hour, talking to me about something I didn't understand— a medication or a test, a good sign or a bad one. I asked as many questions as I could, but they didn't have a lot of news and I didn't have a lot of coherent thoughts. I sat in that chair holding Mac, watching the morning break slowly, pale and cold and bleached of color, over the farmland outside the window. By dawn I felt numb, and I needed pain meds and a change of clothes badly. I had bled through my clothes and hadn't eaten, but I couldn't set Mac down, even for a second.

Aaron was at the pediatrician with Henry, my mom was still trying to get home, and my dad had a day full of meetings. My dad stopped over before his first meeting with clothes that Aaron had packed for me, and I think it was clear to him that I was hanging by a filament, dazed and worn-out. "I think I'll stay," he said calmly, almost in passing. He called his assistant and told her his meetings needed to be rescheduled because I needed him at the hospital.

Even now, months later, that act registers to me as one of his finest parenting moments. I don't know what was written on my face that morning, but I know I needed to not be alone, in the most desperate of ways. I needed someone else to talk to the nurses. I needed someone to tell me to drink some tea, someone to hold Mac for just a minute, someone to field the emails and the calls and the visits. I needed someone to be stronger than I was that day.

At one point, he sent me out of the room. He told me I had to stretch my legs and get something to eat. And he told me not to come back for thirty minutes. He said there was a chapel and suggested I walk down there and also walk outside for some fresh air.

I didn't want to be even an elevator ride away from Mac, and I contemplated standing just outside the room for thirty minutes, but I walked to the chapel. I'd sent a text to my friend Emily, and in her reply, she said that when she's scared about her baby, her mom reminds her to pray to Mary, the Blessed Mother, the one who understands, certainly, what it's like to worry about a child. She said she'd pray the Hail Mary for me and for Baby Mac.

Mary, then, was fresh in my mind, and it didn't seem at all surprising that there was a tall, slender statue of her in the chapel. I knelt near her and looked up at her face, and I prayed almost audibly for our baby. *Dear God, we need your help*, I said. *Help my baby. Help my baby. Help my baby.* No longer a prayer, now more a keening, a low wail. *Help my baby. Help my baby.* The statue of Mary, pale and silent, reminded me that I wasn't alone at all, that I was one of a great line of mothers who entrusted their children into God's care, terrifying as it is. I got up and stood before her, light streaming through the stained glass. I wiped my tears, and I walked back to the elevator.

All of Mac's tests were coming back negative, which was the best possible news. The doctors explained that the tests were sort of like a Polaroid, developing over time. Every three hours, a doctor came in to update me on the lab's findings, and every three hours, the Polaroid got a little clearer. A little good news, every time. His fever was inching down; the results were becoming clearer.

If everything continued in this direction, we could go home on Sunday morning, but if anything changed—his fever rose, he became dehydrated, he lost weight—anything, then he'd stay. I became obsessed with those three-hour reports and with his temperature. I could recite every tenth-of-a-degree change for the nurses, and I nursed Mac constantly, trying to make sure he wouldn't lose weight or become dehydrated. I kept the room as cold as an icebox, trying to keep his fever down, no matter how many times the nurses told me that's not really how it works.

The doctor had told us our final results were coming at 2:00 a.m. "You can go first thing in the morning," she said, "because obviously you don't want to leave in the middle of the night." "I do, actually," I said. "I want to leave the second we're allowed to." I was so afraid something small would change and we'd have to stay even a minute longer. I wanted Mac out of there before that could happen.

And so the kind nurse woke me in the night, clutching the lab results. "They're clear," she said. "Let's get you home." She helped carry our bags down to the side entrance, the one they keep open in the night, where Aaron was waiting for us.

The side entrance was just near the chapel, and as I walked by, I glimpsed Mary's pale face in the glow from the streetlights through the stained glass. I don't know the Hail Mary, but I knew enough for that moment. I nodded at her, like dipping your head before royalty. *Hail Mary, full of grace.*

magical white bean soup

I love food that connects us to good memories, that tells us we're safe, that brings us back to sweeter times on hard days. The British call this "nursery food," and I love that term. Memory and food are inextricably linked, of course, and that's why, when you talk to people about food, there's the food *we say we want*—fancy, sophisticated, highbrow even, and then there's the food *we really want*, especially on difficult days.

Soup, it seems, is the ultimate comfort food—warm, soft, slipping down the throat with ease. We eat soup when we're sick, when we're snowed in, when we're heartbroken, when even cutting and chewing seem too much, when we need to be soothed in some deep way.

Soup is cold-weather-dark-sky food. Soup is peasant food—odds and ends, bits and pieces, a way to stretch a piece of meat or a handful of rice. And the best soups are made, I think, when we treat them as such—earthy, simple, slow, soothing. Soup is the wool sweater, not the little black dress. It's the cardigan with elbow patches, not the pressed shirt and tie.

I love to throw off people's expectations about a meal a little bit. I get so excited about mailed invitations, heels and ties, champagne as you walk in—and then big steaming bowls of braised beef, hunks of bread ripped instead of sliced with a knife, a board of cheese, a bowl of olives—rich, humble, comfort food instead of fiddly fancy food, stacked into towers and surrounded by sauces. I want people to sit down and feel at home, not like there's a scientist in the kitchen but like there's a sister there, someone who loves them, who understands their history and wants to remind them of something lovely, who wants to recall together a sweet time.

Last winter, I cooked up a little dinner party idea. Emily was coming into town from Michigan, and I wanted to connect her with some of my friends, some she'd already met, and some I knew she'd love. Kristi offered to host if I cooked, so we gathered a lovely group of women—two old friends from the city, one of Kristi's best friends, one of my oldest friends, seven total. And quite an assortment of dietary restrictions and preferences: one fish-only vegetarian, one gluten-free and dairy-free, and two pregnant.

So no red meat. Nothing cheesy and comfort-y like lasagna. Most pregnant women aren't wild about sushi. I contemplated a roasted chicken and a homemade mac and cheese—something for everyone. But I wanted something even simpler than that. I was determined to find something everyone could eat together, with minimal changes and instructions. After years of Aaron's gluten-free diet, I know how it feels for everyone else to be eating one thing while one person eats the forlorn gluten-free or vegetarian dish. I wanted us to eat together, from the same bowls, tasting the same flavors.

Enter magical white bean soup. It's vegan, dairy-free and gluten-free, inexpensive, rich and flavorful. For our little dinner party, Kristi served charcuterie and olives before we sat down, and then with the soup, we had a simple mixed green salad with vinaigrette and crusty gluten-free bread. For dessert, Brannon roasted fruit to serve over rice milk ice cream and also served chocolate-dipped shortbread.

I love the familiarity of the same faces around the same table —the inside jokes and the shared histories that have been built, brick by brick, story by story, for years. But at the same time, I also love connecting people from different parts of my life—I loved hearing Emily and Kristi talk about design and architecture, and it was so fun to see Christina and Brannon connect over their mutual commitment to natural cleaning products—even though they did kind of break our hearts by pronouncing almost all of our favorite products highly toxic.

Inevitably, when we gather people together, we bring our values and restrictions to the table with us. Many cooks and food writers have nothing but negative things to say about people who have dietary restrictions or preferences. Quite often it's suggested that you just make what you want to make, and everyone can find something to eat, most likely. But if feeding people around your table is about connecting with them more than it is about showing off your menu or skills, isn't it important to cook in such a way that their preferences or restrictions are honored?

Anyone who cooks will tell you that low-maintenance eaters are the easiest and most fun people to cook for. I've heard several chefs and home cooks say their solution to the problem is to only invite dinner guests who aren't picky, are allergy-free, and who love to eat. For me, that would mean not inviting some of my closest friends and family, and instead having some sort of open-casting call for low-maintenance eaters to fill chairs at my dinner parties. That sounds like a terrible plan.

So over the years, instead of being annoyed at my friends' and guests' proclivities and restrictions, I've tried to look at them as a challenge. Cooking with staples like flour and sugar is easy. Making things taste great with big-flavor items like bacon and cream is a snap. How do I honor and nourish my guests without red meat or dairy or gluten? That's where the challenge begins, and I'm adding this white bean soup to the "can feed almost anyone" list.

We let the soup bubble gently on the stove, and next to the stove we set out little bowls with curls of Parmesan, ribbons of prosciutto, and a tiny pitcher of brightly acidic vinaigrette. As the soup simmered, it got thicker and more flavorful, and a drizzle of the vinaigrette shimmered against the earthiness of the creamy white beans.

We laughed and told stories and let the candles burn down, talking about motherhood and travel, telling labor stories and love stories, learning from each other, asking questions, finding connections. Where else would you want to be on a cold, dark Friday night but around the table?

Magical White Bean Soup

This recipe was inspired by Nancy Silverton's Tuscan White Bean Soup with prosciutto and Parmesan in her cookbook, A Twist of the Wrist.

I liked the idea of a thick bean soup with ribbons of prosciutto (for the meat eaters), a dusting of Parmesan (for the dairy eaters), and a drizzle of balsamic vinaigrette. Even though Nancy's recipe calls for just olive oil, I'm in a serious balsamic phase, and I want it on everything.

Ingredients

2 shallots, sliced
½ pound carrots, sliced into thin coins on a diagonal
1 bulb fennel, sliced
4 celery ribs, sliced on a diagonal
6 cans white beans in liquid (cannellini or great northern beans)
Salt and pepper to taste

Vinaigrette:

    Dijon

    Balsamic vinegar

    Olive oil

For serving:

    Prosciutto, torn into ribbons

    Parmesan, curled into strips with a vegetable peeler

1 tablespoon rosemary, rough chopped

Instructions

In a stockpot or dutch oven, soften two sliced shallots in olive oil over medium heat.

Add carrots, fennel, and celery, and allow to soften, 10 to 15 minutes.

Add beans in their liquid and chopped rosemary.

Cover and cook for 20 minutes at a gentle boil.

Taste, add salt and pepper, taste again—keep in mind that you'll get a good amount of salt from the toppings.

Cook for an additional 20 minutes, or longer if you have time. Off heat, mash with a potato masher or the back of a wooden spoon for a rustic, chunky texture. If you'd like a smoother texture, run it through a food processor or use an immersion blender in the pot.

Balsamic vinaigrette:

Mix a spoonful of Dijon, a few tablespoons of balsamic, a quarter cup or so of olive oil, some salt and pepper in a glass jar, then shake well. Adjust to taste—I usually like a 2:1 ratio of oil to vinegar and Dijon.

Serve with a small pitcher of vinaigrette, and bowls of prosciutto torn into ribbons, curls of Parmesan, and chopped rosemary.

SERVES: 6 to 8

present over perfect

Here we are again, Christmastime.

I'm certainly not the first to point out the irony that it's during Christmastime that we find ourselves most tempted to abandon Christlikeness in favor of overspending, overdoing, and overconsuming, but I find it to be true: the season that centers around the silent, holy night; the simple baby; and the star very quickly becomes the season in which we over-everything— overspend, overeat, overindulge, overcommit, all in the name of celebration.

I fall into it every year, and this particular year, I was falling even a little bit deeper than in previous years because we had a newborn; because my husband was involved in the Christmas services at our church, which meant he was out almost every night in December for rehearsals and programs; and because I had agreed to speak at several events in Atlanta and Dallas, even though it meant taking a nine-week-old with me.

Our week was full to bursting with family parties and gatherings with friends, preschool Christmas programs and coffee dates with out-of-town friends just here for the holidays. Our gifts were mostly purchased but mostly not wrapped, and our laundry situation, after a busy weekend, was dire.

The stress and chaos were on the rise, and something had to change or I'd miss the loveliness of the season entirely. I stopped myself in the middle of it all—the trips, the wrapping, the cookies, the expectations—and I asked for help. I prayed for new eyes to see, for a way outside myself and my tense, swirling chaos. As I slowed down and listened, three words laid themselves on my worn-out spirit like a blanket: *present over perfect*.

A few times a year, I officiate a wedding. It began when one of my best friends asked me to co-officiate her joint-faith wedding ceremony as a representative of her faith. In her words, she wasn't religious yet, but if she ever was, she'd be what I was. I took that as a great compliment, and loved sharing the duties of officiant for her wedding ceremony.

When I officiate a wedding, I usually meet with the bride and groom about a week before, and there are a few pieces of advice I always give. The first is that from that point on, nothing can get added to the wedding to-do list. Things can only be taken off the list—either because they're completed or abandoned. But nothing gets added—no last-minute project, no stroke of genius DIY you saw on Pinterest. If it's not already on the list, no matter how charming, adding it will only make you crazy.

And then I tell them that while *they* can add nothing to the list, I can, in fact, add two very important things to their list. First: a no-wedding-talk date. Second: rest, whatever that means—sleep, an unscheduled hour, a walk, a bath. They always look at me like I'm nuts. I can see them thinking, "We're up to our ears in seating charts and programs to assemble and family drama to mitigate, and you want us to go on a date and then take a nap?"

Actually, yes. Because what will make their wedding day *perfect* is not the flowers or the favors, but a bride and groom who are happy, connected, present, patient.

The same is true at Christmas. I can show up with my *perfectly* wrapped grab bag gift and my *perfectly* baked cookies ... and my *perfectly* resentful and frazzled self, ready to snap at the first family member who looks at me wrong. Or I can choose to rest my body and nourish my spirit, knowing that taking a grounded, present self to each holiday gathering is more important than the gifts I bring.

And so I determined to add nothing to the to-do list. I abandoned well-intentioned but time-consuming projects. And in their place I'm making rest and space priorities, so that what I offer to my family is more than a brittle mask over a wound-up and depleted soul. My intention for this season is *present over perfect.*

As the season has unfolded, I've been given opportunity after opportunity to live this out. A new friend invited me to a cookie exchange on the only night Aaron would be home until Christmas. We didn't have plans, per se, but I had a sense we needed to be home together. And so I said no, which was hard for me, and our little family did approximately nothing, which was exactly what we needed.

I cohosted a party, and one of the things I brought was frozen meatballs. I was planning, of course, to make them from scratch. But it was too much for me, too much time and energy I don't have at this time of the year.

And, *of course*, no one cared. That's the lesson in this for people like me who sometimes get wound up about doing things perfectly: 90 percent of the people in your life won't know the difference between, say, fresh and frozen, or handmade and store-bought, and the 10 percent who do notice are just as stressed-out as you are, and your willingness to choose simplicity just might set them free to do the same.

My friends from high school always get together at Christmas, and in the last several years we've started a tradition of building gingerbread houses with all our kids. This year, two of us had sick kids. I had a newborn. One was working full-time in a new position. One was nine months pregnant. As the emails swirled around about a date for this year, finally Courtney said, "I love you all so much—enough to let tradition slide this year in order to keep things simpler this season." Ah, yes. Yes. *Yes.*

One thing's for sure: if you decide to be courageous and sane, if you decide not to overspend or overcommit or overschedule, the healthy people in your life will respect those choices. And the unhealthy people in your life will freak out, because you're making a healthy choice they're not currently free to make. Don't for one second let that stop you.

Either I can be here, fully here, my imperfect, messy, tired but wholly present self, or I can miss it—this moment, this conversation, this time around the table, whatever it is—because I'm trying, and failing, to be perfect, keep the house perfect, make the meal perfect, ensure the gift is perfect. But this season I'm not trying for perfect. I'm just trying to show up, every time, with honesty and attentiveness.

The irony, of course, must not be lost on us: a season that is, at its heart, a love story—a story about faith and fragility, angels, a baby, a star—that sweet, simply beautiful story gets lost so easily in a jarring, toxic tangle of sugar and shopping bags and rushing and parking lots and expectations.

In our lowest, most fragmented moments, we feel out of control—controlled, in fact, by expectations and to-do lists and commitments and traditions. It's that time of year, we shrug, when things get a little crazy. No avoiding it.

But that's not true. And that's shifting the blame. We have, each one of us, been entrusted with one life, made up of days and hours and minutes. We're spending them according to our values, whether or not we admit it.

When things are too crazy, the only voices I hear are the voices of fear and shame. I stop being able to hear the voice of God, the voice of rest, the voice of hope and healing and restoration, the voice that gives new life to dry old bones. And instead I hear that old song I've heard all my life: *You're not good enough. You're not good enough.*

But that voice is a lie. And it's a terrible guide. When I listen to it, I burn the candle at both ends and try to light the middle while I'm at it. The voice of God invites us to full, whole living—to rest, to abundance, to enough. To say no. To say no more. To say I'm going to choose to live wholly and completely in the present, even though this ragged, run-down person I am right now is so far from perfect.

Let's be courageous in these days. Let's choose love and rest and grace. Let's use our minutes and hours to create memories with the people we love instead of dragging them on one more errand or shushing them while we accomplish one more seemingly necessary thing. Let's honor the story—the silent night, the angels, the miracle child, the simple birth, with each choice that we make.

My prayer is that we'll find ourselves drawn closer and closer to the heart of the story, the beautiful, beating heart of it all, that the chaos around us and within us will recede, and the most important things will be clear and lovely at every turn. I pray that we'll understand the transforming power that lies in saying no, because it's an act of faith, a tangible demonstration of the belief that you are so much more than what you do. I pray that we'll live with intention, hope, and love in this wild season and in every season, and that the God who loves us will bring new life to our worn-out hearts this year and every year, that we'll live, truly and deeply, in the present, instead of waiting, waiting, waiting for perfect.

Bacon-Wrapped Dates

In the spirit of present over perfect, I give you bacon-wrapped dates. These are a go-to, serve-at-every-gathering, take-to-every-party treat. There are only three ingredients; you can make them ahead of time; you can use a foil pan for less cleanup; and, most important, people adore them. Quite often, I feel like I ought to make something impressive and fiddly—a tart with a homemade pastry crust, or something that requires a mandoline or sterilized jars. But then it seems far too complicated, and I find myself reaching for the dates, the goat cheese, the bacon. I keep them all in my freezer, at the ready for those moments when three little ingredients and a little soothing kitchen work can brighten sagging spirits.

I know they may sound like a terrible idea, but stay with me. I ate them for the first time at a tapas restaurant in Los Angeles with my friends Laura and Jeff, and then I made them first for the Cooking Club for tapas night at Amanda's house, quite early in the club's existence—the third month, or possibly the second.

At one point in the night, I went to the bathroom, and as I came out, I heard them all whispering, "They're good! They're actually really, really good. And I thought they'd be terrible!" "I can hear you!" I yelled from the hallway. "And I knew you'd like them."

Brannon confessed several months later that she'd developed a habit of making three or four at a time to eat in the bathtub late at night, and as time went on, I'd get texts or emails from near-strangers: "How do I make those dates again?"

The first time our friend Matt tasted bacon-wrapped dates, he said, "Bacon-wrapped dates? More like bacon-wrapped clouds of heaven!" Exactly.

I'm not going to make a case that they're healthy, or that they're the most practical thing to learn if you're only going to make one recipe from this whole book. (If that's the case, the most practical is risotto or goat cheese scrambled eggs.) But practicality has never been my strong suit, so I think you should make these. Perfect these little numbers, and people will be happy every time you walk in to a party. It's like holding a puppy or a baby—suddenly you become irresistible, which is a great feeling, even if it's just because you're carrying bacon.

Some people call them "devils on horseback." Some people use bleu cheese instead of goat cheese, and also add a walnut. Some people add an almond, which looks too much like a date pit to me. If you must add a nut, make it a pecan. But really? You don't need it. Some people serve them with mango chutney. I adore mango chutney, but seriously—all you need is bacon, dates, and goat cheese.

I prep the dates the night before and put them in a disposable foil pan in the fridge. Then mid-afternoon on the day of the party, I put the foil pan straight into the oven, and when they're done, I let them cool to room temperature on paper towels before plating.

Get ready to be loved.

Ingredients

- 1 8-ounce package pitted dates
- 4 ounces goat cheese
- 1 16-ounce package bacon

Instructions

Slice alongside one side of each date, from the top to the bottom, so you can open it like a tiny book. Scoop a small amount of goat cheese into the center of each one, and then close it back up.

Cut the whole package of bacon in half, so that each long strip is now half as long. Wrap a half-slice of bacon around the outside of each date.

Arrange seam side down in a baking dish or on a baking sheet with sides to catch any grease. A foil pan is really nice for no cleanup.

Bake at 400 degrees for 20 to 25 minutes, or until well browned and crispy. Drain on a paper towel, and serve warm or at room temperature, but definitely not hot, unless you want to burn the roof of your mouth so badly you don't taste anything for days.

the bass player's birthday

Every band should have a bass player like Nathan, and every person should have a friend like Nathan. As a musician, he's that perfect mix of really talented and totally low-key. He's always prepared, always ready to play, and—especially crucial for a bass player—he knows when to play and when to let the spaces and silences create the groove he's looking for. Also, he has the coolest hair of any man I know. Really, all you need to know about Nathan is that he willingly dressed up like Superman for Henry's third birthday party. You have to be a very good person to do that.

As Aaron worked on the band's calendar for the next few months, he realized they were about to schedule a rehearsal on Nathan's thirtieth birthday. Aaron tried to reschedule, but Nathan and his wife, Becky, assured him they were having a party on the weekend, and it wouldn't be a problem to rehearse that night. To feel better about making someone work on the night of such an important birthday, Aaron cut a deal: they'd rehearse, but only if we could have a birthday dinner for him at our house afterward.

I asked Becky about a few foods Nathan likes or things that are special to him—she mentioned mushrooms, risotto, and raspberries. While the band was rehearsing, Becky and I made dinner. We made mushroom and bacon risotto, cooking the mushrooms in bacon fat and a splash of cognac. We trimmed the woody ends off stalks of asparagus to roast with lots of Parmesan and a squeeze of lemon, dressed greens with a simple vinaigrette, and ladled the stock into the risotto bit by bit.

Dinner was lovely—lots of laughter and inside jokes. I've been feeding musicians since I met Aaron nearly thirteen years ago, and I find them some of my favorite people to feed. Some, of course, absolutely live the stereotype of "starving artist," so I've gotten used to packing up every last bit of leftovers and sending them with skinny guitar players and drummers, feeling maternal, knowing I'll never see that container again. And musicians tend to be sense-oriented people, so they notice texture and smell and flavor—the most fun people to feed, of course.

I love that we have a steady stream of musicians in our home, a community of people who believe that art and creativity and soul really matter, that making something out of nothing and telling your story—through lyrics or essays or anything at all—is noble work. That night we ate and talked and laughed. We told stories—best shows we've ever been to, songs that move us, venues they'd love to play someday.

After dinner we moved to the "soft chairs"—one of the great concessions of our marriage. I'm a table person. I like to sit at the table so long that you have to open more wine, so long that after the dessert is gone and the candles are burning down, you get dinner back out and begin to pick at it again with forks, cold and straight out of the pan. Aaron, on the other hand, would like to sit at the table for exactly as long as it takes for everyone to clean their plate, and then immediately adjourn to comfier seating options. This usually takes him about six minutes.

His family is absolutely the same way—all fast eaters who want to leave the table the second they're finished. My brother-in-law Austin, who also married into the family, is a notoriously slow eater, and once at a restaurant the entire family was on their way out to the car, coats on and bill paid, when they realized Austin was only halfway through his meal.

What this means is that there's a complex and wordless negotiation going on between Aaron and me as people begin to finish their meals. About fifteen minutes into the meal, he gives me the "Now?" look and I give him the "What? Already?" look in response. The two other wordless conversations we're always having when we entertain are about volume and temperature. I always, always think the music is too loud and the house is too cold, and he always, always thinks the music is too soft and the house is too hot. I walk by the volume knob and nudge it down, and while I'm at it, swing by the thermostat and inch it up a degree or two. Then while I'm deep in conversation or serving dessert, all at once I notice that I'm freezing and also screaming to hear my own voice—he turned up the music and turned down the heat. The battle rages on.

All this happens without a word and usually without a guest noticing—such is the magic of ten years of marriage. After three or four of Aaron's raised eyebrows, I acquiesce, and we move to the soft chairs for dessert and toasts. Becky told me that Nathan loves raspberries, so I borrowed my cousin Amanda's ice cream maker. I made the simplest vanilla ice cream and added some fresh raspberries halfway through and some more at the very end so it would be striped with pink and also have big chunks of berry.

Birthday toasts began as a tradition we shared with our best friends in Grand Rapids. Each person comes ready to say something about what that person has brought to their life in the last year or a prayer for the year to come, and after dinner, we toast with those thoughts. Aaron and I love the tradition, and we love inviting new friends into it—it feels like a way of honoring something important that our Grand Rapids friends gave to us.

Nathan is the kind of person who is encouraging people all

the time—between songs at rehearsal, in the green room, in conversation. He has a warm, easygoing presence, and people love to be around him. But he's definitely more comfortable encouraging someone else or making a fuss about someone else than being the center of attention. At first when we were sharing, I felt his nervousness, like he wanted us to stop, like he wanted to shift attention to someone else or something else. But we stayed with it, gentle pressure, stories and prayers and words of gratitude. We talked about what he teaches us, what he adds to the band, to our church, to each of our lives.

You could feel the air changing at a certain point, like nobody wanted to move or take a breath or another bite of ice cream. Then a minute later, someone would make a joke and the tension would be broken, but what I remember most about that night are those moments when it was absolutely silent except for one voice, when Ben or Izzy or Becky looked right at Nate and said, "This is something I love about you," or, "This is why I love being in a band with you," or, "This is what you've taught me."

The heart of hospitality is creating space for these moments, protecting that fragile bubble of vulnerability and truth and love. It's all too rare that we tell the people we love exactly why we love them—what they bring to our lives, why our lives are richer because they're in it. We do it best, I think, with our nuclear family —most of us tell our children and spouses how much we love them easily and often. But that night was an unusual and very beautiful thing. We risked the awkwardness of saying tender, meaningful things out loud in front of everyone, in front of our friends, trusting that those words would travel down to a very deep part of someone we cared about. I watched Nathan's face, and I watched it move from slightly nervous and uncomfortable to overwhelmed in the best possible way.

Sometimes food is the end and sometimes it's a means to an

end, and sometimes you don't know which it is until it happens. The food was good that night. I loved being able to serve foods that were meaningful to Nathan, that represented his story and history, and we had a great meal together. But that night wasn't about the food. The food and the table and the laughter helped to create sacred space, a place to give someone the gift of words. That's what the night was about — sacred space and words of love. Well, that and fresh raspberry ice cream.

russian dolls

There's something about our boys right now, about this split-second moment in time, that I want to hold in my heart forever and ever. It's a little nutty, of course. Mac is newly mobile, and while he does have so many lovely qualities, sleeping through the night is totally not his jam. Henry is such a great kid, but also oddly prone to balling up his fists and screaming "No-o-o-o!" to what I think are fairly innocuous requests: take a shower, for instance, or put on clean underwear.

All that to say, they are very real, very normal children, not angels or devils, just children—difficult and sweet and exhausting and wonderful all in the same moment, all the time.

Some of what's making this season so unusually rich is that they both seem to be at those tiny, almost imperceptible hinge points —one thing and also entirely another, changing back and forth breath by breath. Mac is an infant, but you can see flashes of boy, you can see the wheels turning in his little mind, and the moments of discovery couldn't be clearer if they had cartoon lightbulbs above them. He's crawling, discovering the world, telling us who he is and what he wants. He's just starting to reach for me, and to have preferences beyond hungry or tired or cold or hot. He wants this toy or that one, this set of arms or that one. He wants to be traveling, generally, rolling and crawling, pulling up on the coffee table. My mom caught him trying to scale the stairs at her house with his eyes on her, looking at her like, "Do you see what I'm attempting over here? Can you even believe this, Nana?"

I can see the big boy in him, the glimmers of who he's becoming, even though he is still squarely baby, still giggling with his toes in his mouth, still snuggling and squirmy in the bath and sleeping with his little buns in the air. But the boy's in there. I can see him when I'm looking at just the right angle, like a mirage or an optical illusion, a hidden passageway.

With your first baby, or at least with our first baby, you're so excited for them to get big! Big! Big! You want them to do things, to become their big, grown-up selves, to show you that they're geniuses, precocious in every way. But I want to keep Mac tiny. I want him to be my baby forever. I totally might be one of those moms who carries a four-year-old in a BabyBjörn, legs dangling past my knees. I'll keep him in footie sleepers until he's twelve, cut his meat until he has a driver's license. Stay a baby, darling.

I feel like our boys are the perfect ages right now—a big boy and a baby boy. I don't need Mac to get big; I already have a lovely, stinky, adventurous, chatty big boy. That position's been filled, and what I need is for Mac to stay my baby—my tiny, snuggly, smiling baby boy.

But this is perhaps the heart of parenting: despite my aching, desperate baby-love, it's my job to help him into being a big boy. It's my job, my honor, to walk him, quite literally, from baby to toddler to boy to man.

It used to drive me crazy when adults who knew me when I was little always wanted to tell me stories about when I was little, that they couldn't see how all grown-up I was. Some of this, certainly, is the hazard of living and working in your hometown. After I graduated from college, when I started my first job at the church my parents started, I was all full of adultness—dress pants, lipstick, agendas for meetings. And quite routinely in one of these meetings, someone would bring up the fact that they'd changed my diaper. And now everyone's thinking about my baby buns, not my extremely adult professional self.

But now I understand why people who knew me as a child can't ever stop seeing me as a child. Someday, ostensibly, my kids and my friends' kids will be adults with opinions and perspectives and skills. Someday, ostensibly, Annette's son, Spence, or Joe's son, Deacon, will sit across the table from us and share their thoughts about culture or politics or rocket science. And I will try so hard not to say something like, "Spenc-er-iffic, pal, remember when you and Henry jumped on the couch in your matching jammies when we came to visit you in San Clemente? That's right when you were learning to go potty like a big boy!"

It's our job to let them grow up, to let them become big and smart and grown-up, but it's so tempting to keep them little forever, or at least to try. These six months have been the blink of an eye, the season I'd longed for, some of the sweetest months of my life. There's nothing like a first baby, but the second time around has a loveliness all its own, because you know what's coming—you know that this baby, this tiny, odd wild animal will grow into a person with words and ideas and personality.

It's like Michelangelo chipping the block of stone to free the sculpture inside: the grown-up boy is in there, furled tightly like a bud on a branch, unfolding ever so slowly and then sometimes all at once. Now that I know Henry the five-year-old, I can see evidence of this boy all the way back, in his earliest moments: strong, imaginative, full of energy. And so I peer into Mac's little face: Who will you be? What clues are you leaving us even now about the boy inside all that baby?

There's a photo of me on the wall in my parents' house, one of my senior pictures. I picked two I liked, and my mom picked one I thought was weird—my expression was veiled, like I knew a secret, and I didn't look like myself, I didn't think. I liked the ones that were broad smiles, straightforward, happy-looking. But my mom insisted on this other one because she said she had a sense, when she looked at it, of the woman I'd become in the future. And now that I'm a parent, I get it, completely. She was right. That photo looks strangely just like me now, twice the age as when it was taken, and the ones I liked are time capsules of a moment that came and passed in a flash—young, tender, all possibility.

I see flashes of Henry's future face all the time in him, partially because he looks so much like me, and so much, in turn, like my dad. And because he's right on the precipice, the tightrope walk of little boy and big boy. Yesterday at his kindergarten screening I saw both of them—the little boy and the big—in alternating moments. He was shy and proud; he was uncertain and full of swagger. He was little and he was big, right in the same day, right in the same moments.

He was sick over the weekend, and he wanted to sit on my lap and have my arms wrapped around him as tightly as I could. I didn't complain for a second. And then last night as we were driving, he said, "I've been thinking about the bad choices I made today. I'm really sorry, Mom. I'm going to make better choices tomorrow." What more can one expect from any adult than that —better choices tomorrow instead of today? What a big man!

He wears a little Timex, even though he can't tell time, and most days he wears a clip-on tie. His favorite jeans these days are, in his words, "his rock 'n roller skinnies." Seriously. Five might be the perfect age for a human—smart and sweet, the perfect mash-up of little and big. Still full of kisses, but discovering something new about the world every day too.

One thing Aaron and I remind each other about all the time is that kids aren't vanity projects, and they're not extensions of our own images. This is especially helpful when Henry goes to school in rainbow-striped pajama bottoms, cowboy boots, and a Chicago Bears sweatshirt that doesn't quite fit over his belly. He's a person, not a paper doll. And we're his parents, not his marketing team.

My grandma is eighty-two, and I love to look at old photographs of her and my grandpa. She told me one morning while we were flipping the pages of an album that getting old is like carrying all these selves with you. She said she remembers just how that thirteen-year-old in the picture felt, and how that nineteen-year-old bride felt, and how that thirty-year-old on the back of a motorcycle felt. She said you carry them inside you, collecting them along the way, more and more and more selves inside you with each passing year, like those Russian dolls, stacking one inside the other, nesting within themselves, waiting to be discovered, one and then another.

The other night I was folding laundry in the basement and my eye fell on a crate of framed photos that used to be on display but got displaced for baby photos or more recent family pictures. I dug out one old photo of Aaron and myself and put it on the buffet next to our wedding photo and pictures of the boys. Aaron was delighted. "I love that photo," he said. "I love remembering who we were then."

We were at a wedding, right after we had started dating, and you can tell by the way his arm is around me so tightly, by the way I'm huddled into him so closely, that if I could have climbed on to his lap, I would have, that if we could have kissed throughout the entire reception, we would have.

Tomorrow we're going to a wedding, and in some sort of super-weird coincidence, I'm wearing the dress I wore in that photo all those years ago. This time the wedding's in Los Angeles, and we'll fly out there with our sleepy children, arriving at our friends' house late at night, carrying sleeping kids and a diaper bag and a Superman backpack full of toys.

But we're still that couple in the photo, and maybe we'll find them again just for a moment. Maybe on the dance floor, maybe as we hold hands for the vows — I always want to hold hands, and I always cry, and Aaron always shakes his head and laughs at me. We fell in love, really, in LA on what was supposed to be a work trip. We drove all day, interviewing people from San Diego to Santa Barbara, mile after mile after mile in the sunshine, and here we are again, thirteen years later, getting ready to rent a car and buckle two boys into car seats, the greatest evidence of the life we've made along the way.

But when I look at that photo, when I look at that dress, when I think of the LA highway we drove so many years ago, the same one we'll travel tomorrow, I don't see the kids and the car seats and all the ways we've changed. What I see is a girl who was wild about a boy, and a boy who loved that girl right back. And it makes me happy to know they're still in there, still inside us, like Russian dolls.

on scrambled eggs
and doing hard things

After Mac was born, my neighbor Lindsay brought over a pan of enchiladas and Jessie made an amazing pumpkin apple cake. Jenny brought us Smitten Kitchen's baked potato soup and Brannon brought Barefoot Contessa's boeuf bourguignon. We went to Dallas and had great pizza from Fireside Pies and a fantastic Tex-Mex lunch at Chuy's. Wonder of wonders, I was not losing the baby weight as rapidly as I expected.

I want to be the kind of person who makes peace with her body. Also, I want to fit into my pants. Not size-two pants. Not Barbie pants. Just, you know, very average-sized jeans from the Gap. I want to live with peace and confidence, without deprivation and shame, and while I'm being honest, I want to retire the maternity yoga pants that, unfortunately, I'm still wearing because they're the only ones that fit. I don't want to live by rules and regulations, but I also don't want to be ruled by my appetites.

I resist and kick at discipline every chance I get, and then when I break down and do something hard, I find that it builds something in me, that it makes me stronger, not just in that area but in all sorts of areas. So for years I was a dieter, a shame-laden hider, fearful and vibrating with self-loathing. Then I was an eater, finally letting myself make peace with my appetites, wary and defensive about any attempt to limit or control.

And now these days, I'm something else, something new. I try to feed myself with care and attentiveness, without shame, without punishment. In some seasons, I choose discipline, not because I'm out of control, not as a punishment, but because it heals me, helps me, and builds and resets something good inside me. And because if I had to wear those maternity yoga pants for one more day, I thought I'd lose my mind.

I believe in the back and forth rhythm of feasting and fasting, but I was having a little trouble clicking over into fasting, stuck for a little too long on the feasting side of things, so I signed up for a six-week nutrition and exercise program with my friend Robin. She's a Pilates instructor in the Bay Area, and her whole deal is a pro-balance, anti-guilt attitude toward nutrition and fitness. I love this. As you may imagine, there are certain fitness types that I have trouble connecting with. Like ... most of them. I don't like to be yelled at; I don't like drinking protein shakes; and deprivation sends me into a rebellious tailspin.

But I needed something, and I trusted Robin's perspective, so I signed up. I did Pilates videos; I ate lots of quinoa and white beans and loads of fresh produce; and I emailed Robin whenever I felt like what I really wanted was a wheelbarrow full of nachos, or when the last thing I wanted to do was a Pilates video in a hotel room at midnight.

In the fourth week of the six-week plan, however, on a spectacular spring Wednesday, I hit my moment. If you've ever given anything up—dieted or quit smoking or given up something for Lent—you know that moment, the one when you desperately, deeply want to abandon the plan, when you're just absolutely certain you'll feel endlessly better if you just get what you want instead of all this staying-in-line virtuous nonsense.

I still can't totally figure out what got me to the moment, although perhaps we can lay as a foundation the fact that our sweet six-month-old was not sleeping through the night. Mac has so many lovely skills, like smiling and being darling, but sleeping was not in his repertoire at that point. Layer on to this the fact that I had a writing deadline for a project I was very excited about but was not by any stretch close to finishing. Another layer: all of a sudden my calendar went crazy, and I was speaking at no less than nine events before the writing project deadline, and all nine of them required new content.

A few more layers: Aaron's work schedule was, shall we say, somewhere between full and bonkers that month, and Henry had the energy of a Labrador puppy and also the mess-making ability.

Things started out OK on that particular bright Wednesday, but the cracks started to show early. Henry insisted on bringing his light saber to the grocery store, tucked into his belt, which meant that when he walked next to me, it hit me in the ankles with every step, and all through the store I had to curb my impulse to grab it and throw it as hard and as far as I could. But when we got back, I settled him in with a movie and nursed Mac while I had a conference call. Mac took a good nap and I got a little work done, and then we went to Casey's for a playdate.

It should have been glorious—I mean, I think it was glorious for everyone else. The babies rolled around on a blanket and the big kids played on the swings, and Casey picked up barbecue from the Texan—turkey and spicy beans and coleslaw, lemonade and grapes and hot dogs for the kids.

But Mac was fussing and teething, and Henry was experiencing lots of light-saber-related frustration—not thrilled to be sharing it with Jack, getting hit with it too hard, and then, in a disastrous downturn, the all-important light saber got broken, and he was hysterical. He cried and then went to sit under a neighbor's tree, so I dragged the fussy, squirmy baby all the way over there to see what I could do.

By the time I got there, Jack had persuaded Henry to keep playing. There was hope after all. When we left, though, Henry didn't listen, and ran away from me and stood in the middle of the road while trying to repair the broken light saber. I yelled at him to get out of the road, and then I yelled at him again in the car: *Stop talking about the light saber. No more. I'm sorry it's broken. I can't fix it. Stop talking about it right now.*

He was silent for a moment, and then he said, in a small, testing-the-waters voice, "Mom? Can I talk about a *different* light saber?" He had me there, but I was so frustrated I wanted to pull over the car and scream. By the time we got home, I was almost in tears, bleary and so tired I felt beat-up.

This is the heart of the story, or the point, rather: What I wanted in that frustrated, depleted, desperate moment was relief. Fifteen years ago, that would have meant a pack of cigarettes, one after the other, blowing the smoke out with some violence, throwing pebbles absently or picking grass from the cracks in the sidewalk. Ten years ago, or eight maybe, it would have meant a staggeringly strong cocktail, harsh and dizzying. A vodka soda, maybe, but hold the soda. But these days, or at least this day, I wanted to eat.

Not to have an approved, healthy, small portion of, say, salmon with broccoli or chard. Not to nibble a few raw almonds while I stretch and slice some veggies. I wanted to do some damage— pizza, maybe, or a burger with melting cheese and sweet potato fries, or a club sandwich. Cold pasta, bread and cheese, chips and dip.

I was almost scared by how badly I wanted an escape hatch out of my feelings, and how trapped and all the more angry I felt that my fancy little Pilates plan wasn't allowing me what I wanted. I felt like kicking someone in the shins just to feel that satisfying thunk.

But this is what I did: When we got home, I asked Aaron to help —to hold the baby while I scrambled some eggs, slowly pushing the soft curds around the pan with a wooden spoon. I added goat cheese and flaked rosemary salt and scooped them from the pan onto a mound of quinoa. I got myself a tall glass of water, and I sat down on the living room floor and ate my eggs.

I did some dishes and read a little and allowed my husband to put me to bed at nine o'clock, and as I was falling asleep, I realized that I had made it through a little something—that if there was ever a moment when I was going to go screaming off my little health plan, that was the one.

I tend to think that when everything is going well, I have the margin to do hard things, to make good choices—to read instead of watch TV, to eat well instead of eat poorly, to engage in deep conversation instead of chatter about other people.

But it's really the opposite, isn't it? It's the making of those harder, better choices right while everything's a mess that makes the mess a little more manageable. I wanted every pizza in the state of Illinois last night. But this morning I would have had to add a sense of failure to my already bruised spirits. I'm not saying I woke up feeling all better. But I do know I could have made it so much worse, that I could have added self-loathing to my tiredness, and that wouldn't have made it easier to bear.

I'm realizing this after what seems like a lifetime of saying to myself, "Well, you can't be expected to do something hard on a day like this, can you?" I did expect more from myself, and I did do something hard, and I'm thankful.

Goat Cheese Scrambled Eggs

I am a very low-key, rules-averse, non-exact cook, but I have strong feelings about scrambled eggs. It's one of the only things I'm truly high-maintenance about. If we're talking about cold, rubbery eggs, I'd rather just have toast. But few things make me happier than a pan of rich, just barely cooked-through, perfectly loose and luscious eggs.

What I've learned along the way is that it's all about a cold pan and low heat. When a friend of ours was teaching his wife to drive their boat, he said this is all you need to know: Slow is cheap. And the same is true with scrambled eggs. The only way you can mess them up, really, is by trying to go too fast, and by cooking them at too high a temp.

Ingredients

  12 eggs, beaten well
    1 4-ounce container crumbled goat cheese

Instructions

I wait until almost everything is done—quinoa is ready, sausages are cooked, tea is steeped, juice is poured. At the very, very last second, the eggs.

Pour the beaten eggs into a cold nonstick pan over low heat, and cook so low that you think, really, *nothing is happening.*

Over time, drag your spatula through the middle, and you'll see some fluffy curds beginning to form.

Steady and slow, now. Slow is cheap.

Run your spatula around the edge of the pan, finding more lovely golden curds.

Keep dragging the spatula back and forth, around the edges, and when it seems like they're about a minute from being done, no longer liquid but just barely solid, turn off the stove, and add a handful of crumbled goat cheese, reserving a little bit to sprinkle on the top.

Serve immediately, like, right that second.

SERVES: 4

happy new year

I've always had visions of a really great New Year's Eve party—
fancy and fun, glamorous and stylish, with flutes of champagne
and kisses at midnight. And every year, we're away with my family.
I'm certainly not complaining. I love our strange little traditions,
but it's more of a foul-weather-gear and flip-flops affair. There is
decidedly no fancy dress, no sparkly jewelry, no mile-high shoes.

So this year, I decided to laugh in the face of the calendar and
have a New Year's Eve party on the 21st of January. I invited friends
and began to obsess about the menu, one of my very favorite
parts of party planning. I read eleven cookbooks at a time and
pore over recipes online. It feels like a big story problem—if this,
then this. That entrée with that vegetable. No, scratch that, those
flavors are perfect with that starter. Begin again. My husband,
after I'd asked him for the zillionth time how he felt about figs or
something, said, "I really wish you got paid hourly to do that."

We had decided to have our house painted early in the month
—it would take one week, tops. But our painter turned out to have
lots of great ideas and lots of the necessary skills, so what began
as paint and wallpaper mushroomed into taking down cabinets
and posts, ripping out and replacing ceilings, adding custom
cabinets, removing a wall of mirrors, and hanging lighting fixtures.

Tom, our painter-turned-general contractor became a regular
fixture in our house and at one point stayed all night to hang

the wallpaper. Sometimes I set out cookies and milk for him, or tiramisu if I went out for lunch at an Italian restaurant. It seemed that if things were going well, he listened to classic rock, but if things were getting a little hairy, he switched to worship music. Understandable, I think.

As the party date neared, Tom worked faster and faster, longer and longer. On the afternoon of the party, his paint cans and tools were on one half of the kitchen counter, while my cutting board and knives and bowls were on the other. At one point that afternoon, Lindsay, who had made the invitations, brought over menu cards and ended up helping Tom screw in outlet plates while I wrestled half a dozen lobsters out of their shells. That's above and beyond, right there, when the graphic designer you've met twice drives an hour to bring menu cards and then gets roped into home repair while she's there.

The party began at seven, and at four, Tom was still working, and I was destroying a carrot soufflé and flinging lobster tails around my half of the kitchen. I made an emergency call to my brother. He came over two hours before the party to help Aaron re-hang curtains and help me with dishes. Best brother ever.

I have a policy of trying new recipes for dinner parties —it's not a performance; it's a meal, and I like trying new things. This thinking usually works in my favor, but I had grossly underestimated the prep time required and was, as they say, seriously in the weeds.

I made a lobster-and-mango salad with Thai flavors, using lobsters Aaron and Todd had speared on our recent trip—lots of ginger and chili, a fair bit of fish sauce, and a very time-consuming julienne of cucumbers. Are there two harder items to prep than mangoes and lobsters? Slippery skins, pits, shells, veins. I whacked away at them, watching the clock.

I'm not the most meticulous of cooks, but even for me, this

was a poor showing. I was off my game, scrambling, messy, shortcutting. For the main course, I made Barefoot Contessa's Indonesian ginger chicken. I had visions of rich, lacquered chicken pieces, burnished almost, but I crowded the pans, and instead they were mealy and pale. I served them over curried jasmine rice that I overcooked by about a half hour, and a carrot soufflé that looked exactly like a pan of brownies.

We also had sugar snap peas with black sesame seeds and dark sesame oil that, thankfully, even I could not mismanage. For dessert, we had vanilla ice cream with shards of dark chocolate sea salted toffee, one of my favorite things in the world. And since I'd made it in advance, my bad kitchen juju that afternoon couldn't mess it up.

As people arrived, we served champagne with goat cheese, fig jam, and prosciutto on crusty bread. That's just about my all-time favorite combination—sharp, bubbly, rich, salty. Earlier in the evening I had been forced to consider the distinct possibility that the entire main course would be inedible, but I soothed myself with the knowledge that there was more than enough champagne and a lovely platter of cheese and jam. We wouldn't starve.

It's easy, when you love parties and love planning, to start thinking of them like little stage productions, each moment just so. I thought twelve of us would sit at my perfect table, arriving just on time, laughing and eating perfectly prepared food.

But I wanted my brother there, and that made us an inelegant thirteen. Then Brian and Jorie told me they were coming late, and at different times. Then Matt and Kristi had to go to a funeral. Then the house was a last-minute mess and I overcooked the rice. The chicken was unsightly. I destroyed a soufflé. And then our first guest came without his wife and with a fresh heartbreak.

Paul is a warm, boisterous South African. He wore a dark suit jacket and handed me a bottle of champagne after he hugged me. We asked where his wife, Deirdre, was, and he put both hands on the counter and looked down for a moment before he looked back up. The week before, they'd told us about her pregnancy—after many, many years of infertility, and their daughter conceived through in vitro, Deirdre was pregnant—totally naturally, totally surprisingly, totally happily. But they'd just come from the doctor with bad news. It looked like the pregnancy wasn't viable, and they'd know more next week.

All Deirdre wanted was to be at home, to cry and curl up and not face a soul. But all Paul wanted was to sit around the table with people who loved him and who could sit with him in the darkness. He said he needed to cry, but that he also needed to laugh, and that he was thankful to be there.

Before we prayed for the meal, Paul filled everyone in on the appointment, and we prayed for them as we thanked God for the meal and for the gift of gathering around the table.

In the invitations, we'd asked each person to come ready to talk about their greatest blessing of the last year and to share a resolution for the year to come. Lindsay had printed tiny cards that slid into tiny envelopes on the back of each invitation, one for each blessing and resolution. I had imagined a rich, lingering conversation, but because we'd started it too late, halfway through the conversation, two couples had to leave to relieve sitters. And I can't remember why, but we started with our resolutions instead of our blessings, and we never did get to talk about the blessings.

Jorie came mid-dinner, and Brian came later than that, straight from a seminary class. They both slipped right into the conversation, and I warmed plates for them, pushing aside place cards and menus. Matt and Kristi came from a funeral after eleven. We moved chairs around and warmed plates for them while they told us about the service.

The night wasn't even close to what I'd pictured, and the table was a wreck, like musical chairs, with people coming and going and switching seats all evening, but this is the thing: it was perfect. It was just as it should have been, and nothing close to what I could have planned. And that's what makes a good party—when the evening and the people and the conversation and the feeling in the room are allowed to be whatever they need to be for that night.

We have a friend who really wants things to be fun. So much so, in fact, that I finally grumbled to my husband mid-fun at one of our friend's events, "It's not fun if you have to manhandle us!" I think it bothered me so much because, like all things that make us crazy, it reminded me way too much of myself. I've overthought, overplanned, and manhandled so many parties and meals over the years.

I distinctly remember hosting Easter for my in-laws the first year we lived in our Michigan house. I had fretted over the menu, the seating chart, the dishes. I cooked a ham, even though I don't know the first thing about it, and to be honest, I hate it. I wrangled everyone to the table, sent out all the other dishes, and when I took the ham out of the oven and put it on the platter, I realized it was completely ice-cold in the middle. And right there, holding the heavy ham in my kitchen as I looked out toward the full dining room, I burst into tears.

The best part of this story is that my in-laws are totally easygoing about stuff like that. I could have said, "Oh, hey, it's going to be another half hour. My fault." They would have turned on the TV or chatted good-naturedly. They're the least critical, hustling, time-conscious people ever. But I was wound up so tightly, wanting to please, wanting to be perfect.

In entertaining, as in every area of life, there are experts and rock stars, people who give us complexes and make us afraid, who load us up with expectations and set impossibly high standards so that most of us give up and the rest of us feel terrible about ourselves when we inevitably fall short.

But entertaining isn't a sport or a competition. It's an act of love, if you let it be. You can twist it and turn it into anything you want—a way to show off your house, a way to compete with your friends, a way to earn love and approval. Or you can decide that every time you open your door, it's an act of love, not performance or competition or striving. You can decide that every time people gather around your table, your goal is nourishment, not neurotic proving. You can decide.

Lots of times I don't get it right, and the vision I have in my head looms larger than the sweet, imperfect story unfolding right in front of me. That New Year's party was shaping up to be an epic production on my part—fancy invitations, lobster and champagne, cool new wallpaper. I felt it coming, the pressure and the performance. This could have been a show—brittle smile, jangled nerves, pushing and pulling and pressuring people to act perfectly in my production. But it wasn't. Maybe it was the sheer chaos level that brought me back down to table, love, friendship. Maybe it was years of regrets at the end of a night when I knew the party had been little more than an exercise in control, not true hospitality or soul.

Whatever the reason, I felt like a bit player that night, not a puppeteer. I laughed and listened and apologized for the food, even though no one really cared. It was a perfectly imperfect night, a sweet and special beginning to a new year—just a few weeks late.

Dark Chocolate Sea Salted Toffee

Every toffee recipe I've read says you need a candy thermometer. I don't have one. I meant to borrow one, but I got impatient late one night and tried the toffee anyway. You know what? We were fine without that pesky candy thermometer. Just keep an eye on the toffee. Keep stirring like you're tending to a very finicky risotto. For a while it's melted butter yellow, sort of popcorn-colored, but then there's a very definite turn, right around the 8- or 9-minute mark, when the soft yellow blooms into amber. That's your moment—when it turns caramel-colored, like cappuccino almost. Turn off the heat and pour. And don't try to eat it off the spoon at that point, whatever you do. I speak from experience, of course.

I find that the toffee gets a little melty if you leave it out on the counter, so I keep it in the fridge and serve a little plate of it after dinner with vanilla ice cream and coffee.

Ingredients

1 cup butter (2 sticks)
2 cups sugar
1 cup dark chocolate chips
1 teaspoon coarse sea salt

Instructions

In a saucepan, combine butter and sugar, and bring to a boil. Over medium-high heat, keep stirring until it turns a deep amber color.

Remove from heat and pour onto a rimmed baking sheet lined with parchment paper. Refrigerate at least 30 minutes, or until cool and solid to the touch.

Melt chocolate chips in a glass bowl over a pot of gently boiling water. When the chocolate is smooth, pour it over the toffee and spread with a spatula. Sprinkle sea salt, and then refrigerate until cooled and solid. Break into irregular pieces.

swimming in silence

In mid-February, which in Chicago is about the time you begin despairing that you will never be warm again, Ryan and Emily invited us to join them in Mexico—seven adults, five kids, a swimming pool right at the house. What could be lovelier? *Nothing*, says this Chicagoan. Absolutely nothing.

We left early on a Wednesday morning. I got our flight departure time wrong, so the morning was a fire drill, flinging things into the car, pleading with the woman at the ticket counter to let us jump the line. We arrived at the gate, miraculously, and we met our friends there, hugging and juggling babies. As the plane descended a few hours later, we looked out into the mountains and the desert, as far as you could see, and then all at once the ocean, navy and severe.

In the van on the way to the house, we stopped for ice-cold Mexican Cokes, supersweet, and peanuts with salt and lime, our first bites of Mexico. After we arrived, we filled up baskets at the market: juice for the kids, bottles of Pacifico, salsa with loads of onion and a bright tangle of cilantro—the red, white, and green of the Mexican flag almost in equal measure.

We went to bed early most nights, and the evenings settled into a loose routine of baths for kids, dinner for kids, bedtime for kids, and then dinner for us. Often, by the time dinner for us came around, we nibbled a few bites of whatever and wandered to bed, tired from the sun and the kids and the swimming.

One clear day we had fish tacos and buckets of beer as we overlooked the boats down at the marina. Another hot, cloudless morning, we went whale watching, and the sight of their huge, slippery bodies cutting the surface of the sea never failed to amaze us. The boys went fishing early one morning and came back with a sierra mackerel, so Ryan extemporized a fantastic ceviche —grapefruit juice, diced tomatoes and pineapple, lots of salt.

Some friends recommended an organic farmers market, so we set out one morning to find it. We were given various sets of confusing, inaccurate, and downright wrong directions that took us all over town—to a flea market, a grocery store, a church, and both ends of the marina, until finally we flagged down a couple with a shopping bag who directed us very specifically to a residential neighborhood in the hills above the marina, across a parking lot, past a house with a pit bull and a hot tub in an old Cadillac. For real, a pit bull and a hot tub in an old Cadillac.

The kids were hot and dusty, and we were tired of dragging them around, so when it turned out that the vegetable market was held in the courtyard of a juice bar and café, we claimed the biggest table and settled in happily for cucumber grapefruit juice and almond coconut muffins and lattes.

We bought loaves of crusty round bread and granola, tamales and poblano crema, and absolutely fantastic tuna. As is always the case for me at farmers markets, I intended to buy herbs and lettuces and left with baked goods and cheese, but such is life, and certainly such is vacation.

For dinner that night we seared the tuna and served it over white rice with little puddles of the poblano crema. The next night, we had the tamales—some with poblanos, some with black beans, some with spicy pork, the richness of the filling perfect against the sweetness of the corn. The nights were mild and cool, and we slept well, worn-out from the day and, of course, from the children.

In the mornings, we tiptoed around, hoping everyone else's kids were still sleeping. I'd slip upstairs to start the coffee and bring down breakfast in bed, slicing a dense loaf of market bread, setting out a pat of butter under a stainless bowl, warming almond milk to pour into dark fragrant Mexican coffee, day breaking slowly and quietly.

Some mornings, our little family would head down to the market and the courtyard, closer to the sea, near the tiny chapel and the both foreign and familiar sounds of daily Mass. The courtyard was lined with rocking chairs with leather seats, and Mac would nap on one of our chests while we rocked and people-watched and drank strong lattes, and while Henry purchased his favorite new thing, a Kinder Surprise—a hollow chocolate egg with a toy inside.

He wasn't tremendously interested in the chocolate, but he loved the toys inside, and he walked carefully and purposefully across the courtyard to the market with a handful of coins and stood in line like a big kid, waiting to make his purchase. The first time he did it, I was standing right outside the market, peering in the bakery window, but as the week went on, and he grew more confident, I stayed in my leather rocker, watching him from across the courtyard, and he walked with extra swagger, like a big kid.

When we first arrived in Mexico, we realized our phones didn't work unless we wanted to pay a fortune in data roaming charges, and my email didn't work on the desktop at the house. What that meant is that I checked my email on my phone every morning for a few costly minutes, just to see if anything pressing had come up, but other than that, we did things the old-fashioned way: we left each other notes and set meeting places.

We sometimes missed each other, but there was something

absolutely fantastic about saying things like, "I'll see you when I get back." Or, "they went for a walk, and maybe they'll be back in an hour." No constant texts, no calls back and forth from the grocery store, no check-in about whether the baby was still sleeping. And beyond that, no Twitter, no Facebook, no blog reading.

Before the trip, I'd spent several weeks in a coffee shop with a laptop, hyperconnected all the time, and the silence of Mexico and my useless phone felt cavernous. I felt a little jumpy, like something really major might be happening and I might miss it. But as time went on, I realized that the really major things were happening all around me, and that more often than not, I had been missing them because my phone had become an extension of my hand, and what it said to people, essentially, is that just being with them isn't enough. This view of the ocean? Not enough. Your story? Not enough.

I'm not antitechnology, of course. But what I realized that week is that in the world we live in now, vacation isn't always about a change of venue. We travel a lot for both fun and our work, and we love it, but we always, always have phones, laptops, iPads. No matter where we are, we're as connected as we are at home, sometimes more so, because we have more free time.

And like more and more people, I think, we don't work in offices or conventional workplaces, where we have set hours we're working and hours we're not. There are so many good things that go with that—flexibility, freedom, lots of time with our kids. At the same time, though, we've realized it means we're sort of working all the time. Aaron will get out of bed to run down to the studio to listen to a mix a producer sends him. I get emails about upcoming events while I'm nursing or at a museum or watching Henry's soccer practice.

The best part about blending all those boundaries is also the worst part about blending all those boundaries: we're always connected to everyone all the time. While I'm face-to-face with my grandmother, my phone is vibrating with Facebook comments or emails from J.Crew. When I'm in Dallas, I'm texting a friend in Reno and answering a question for my editor in Eugene and sending a photo to my mother-in-law back home.

That's good, for lots of reasons. But what I found in Mexico is that being everywhere was keeping me from being anywhere, from being in any one very particular place. All of a sudden, that silence —that blessed, glorious, strange silence—let me be completely in one place. I was totally there, totally in it, without feeling like my mind was divided into a thousand small splinters, spinning out all over the world, leaving nothing but a glassy stare and twitchy fingers always reaching for my phone.

The week in Mexico was amazing—I mean, of course it was: the wide glittering sea everywhere you look, babies and kids, swimming and tacos and limes and laughter and people we love. But it was magical on a deeper level too, because it created in me an appetite for silence that I hadn't tasted for years, possibly. It was like going on a juice fast for your brain, and as much as you're starving, you feel strong and whole and healthy and clear for the first time in a long time. It was unnatural and I liked it, and I think back to that week often, to how non-fragmented my brain and spirit felt, how little I missed on Pinterest and Facebook. I think about how valuable it is to live the life in front of you, regardless of how tempting it is to press your face to the glass of other people's lives online, even though doing that is so much safer and so entirely addictive.

It could have been the ocean—the Pacific and the Sea of Cortez coming together right at the southernmost point, navy and deep, whales breaching and sleek sport fishers zigzagging the coastline. It may have been the warmth of the sun in midday and the soft coolness of morning and night. It may have been the beer with fat wedges of lime, the salsa from the market, thick with cilantro and loads of diced onion. It may have been the sounds of our children in the pool, yelping and splashing. It may have been the seared tuna over rice and poblano crema, or the heavy, almost bitter lattes we drank in the mornings in leather rocking chairs while the sun climbed silently. It could have been any of those things. But I do believe that what made this trip feel more deeply restful than any in recent memory was that it was truly quiet, that the constant chatter and conversation and mental clutter we create with Twitter and Facebook and Pinterest and blogs was, for one week, blessedly silent.

I'm responsible for both creating and consuming all that clutter and noise. I'm a noise person, both literally and figuratively. I'm a multitasker—TV on, magazine open, fridge open, kids chattering, texting one friend, emailing another. All the while I've got something in the microwave and something else bubbling on the stove. My mom is stopping over and the dryer is buzzing, and that's how I like it.

But all of a sudden, on this trip, there was no noise. There was no other conversation to be a part of, nothing happening in the lives of my friends from high school or college or Grand Rapids to overshadow or overtake what we were doing. And largely, what we were doing was nothing in the best possible way. After a few days, I realized how much I liked it. How much the silence sounded like music, and how much better I liked my own life in that silence.

It's easier, of course, to allow yourself to be totally present when you're looking out on the ocean or scanning the shoreline for whales—and, admittedly, when your phone doesn't work anyway. It's a lot harder when you're home, again; when you're with the kids, again; when they're not napping, again; and they're watching *The Backyardigans*, again. I'll do almost anything to not be completely present when I'm surrounded by laundry and the baby won't nap. I don't want to be even partially present when I'm staring down a deadline, shoulder muscles clenched, caffeine making me both blurred and twitchy. We fragment our minds for a reason, of course—because we like the idea of being sixty-seven other places instead of the one lame, lonely place we find ourselves on some days.

But when I think back to Mexico, I force myself to lay down my phone for a while. And I trust that some of what made that time so magical had nothing to do with the lime and the cilantro and the whales, and everything to do with the willingness to be entirely there. I practice, since that trip, being entirely where I am, glamorous or not, and what I find is that it's better to be in one place, wholly and full-heartedly, than a thousand splintery half-places, glamorous as they may be.

Esquites/Mexican Grilled Corn

There are a million ways to make esquites, and my favorite is from Bien Trucha in Geneva. Once when I picked up takeout, I didn't let the fact that I had no utensils stop me from tipping the takeout container straight into my mouth while driving.

Ingredients

- 12 ears of corn
- ½ cup mayonnaise
- ½ cup Cotija or feta cheese, crumbled
- Juice from half of a lime
- ¼ teaspoon cayenne
- Cilantro

Instructions

Shuck the corn, removing both husks and silks, and then soak the ears in water for at least 30 minutes. This keeps them from burning on the grill.

Grill on high for 8 to 10 minutes, turning often. What you're looking for is a mix of char and deep yellow kernels. When the corn is done, allow it to cool, and then cut the kernels off the ears.

Mix together mayonnaise, Cotija cheese, lime juice, and cayenne, adjusting to taste. Mix with corn, and garnish with cilantro before serving.

SERVES: 6 to 8

part four

Food and cooking are among the richest subjects in the world. Every day of our lives, they preoccupy, delight, and refresh us. Food is not just some fuel we need to get us going toward higher things. Cooking is not a drudgery we put up with in order to get the fuel delivered. Rather, each is a heart's astonishment. Both stop us dead in our tracks with wonder. Even more, they sit us down evening after evening, and in the company that forms around our dinner tables, they actually create our humanity.

ROBERT FARRAR CAPON, *The Supper of the Lamb*

what money can't buy

On a clear, cool Saturday morning, the Cooking Club girls arrived at Casey's house. It was early, and the mist was still settled heavily on the grass. We clutched our coffees, murmured hello, and began sliding folding tables out of the garage, stacking clothes and toys, and rolling garment racks of dresses down the driveway, still sleepy and wondering what on earth we'd gotten ourselves into.

More accurately, what I'd gotten us into. I was the one who thought it would be a great idea to have a huge garage sale and bake sale to benefit our church's Care Center. I was the one who insisted it would be so good for us to live with less stuff, and to part with some of it for a good cause. I was the one who put the date on the calendar, and now I was the one everyone was cursing under their breath, dreading the process of dealing with all this stuff.

We'd gathered at Casey's earlier in the week to start sorting through the loads of things we'd been delivering to her basement for over a month. At one point, completely surrounded by mountains of bags and boxes, Margaret said, "I'm going to go ahead and just say it: this is not really my wheelhouse." Not mine either, certainly. After a garage sale in Grand Rapids, I swore I'd never do one again, because I'm truly terrible at it. I like the idea of it, and then I hate all the actual sorting of all the actual things, and when it's sale time, I want it all gone so badly that I slash prices an hour after opening and try to give everything away and close down shop around lunchtime.

This time around, I was hoping the bigger picture would motivate me to better behavior. Because we were giving all the proceeds to the Care Center at our church, the sale would help people right in our neighborhoods feed their families. For more than thirty years, our church has been giving food to families in immediate need all over our city. More than eight hundred volunteers serve regularly at the Care Center, walking families through the aisles, helping them choose bread and meat and vegetables that have been grown in our church's Giving Garden.

Maybe it's because I'm a food person. Maybe it's because I'm a mom. Maybe it's because I've volunteered at the Care Center and have looked into the eyes of moms just like me, moms who live in my town, who have come for groceries because without them they can't feed their families. Whatever the reason, hunger moves me. It upsets me and makes me angry. It gets me all wound up and I want to make it right.

I want to make sure the kids I see at the Care Center always have full bellies, that the church community is meeting their needs in daily, practical, immediate ways. The church is at its best, in my view, when it is more than a set of ideas and ideals, when it is a working, living, breathing, on-the-ground, in-the-mess force for good in our cities and towns.

The last several times the Cooking Club has gathered, we've talked about hunger. We're food people, obviously. We're moms and aunts and sisters. We care about hunger, and we wanted to find a tactile, practical way to make a difference in our town. And as we talked about hunger, about privilege and simplicity and waste and wealth, we talked about how easy it is to settle into a lifestyle of accumulation, to get used to buying and buying and buying, and then living in homes that are bursting with stuff we don't need, can't find a place for, shouldn't have bought in the first place. We want to live simpler, more responsible lives, with less waste and clutter. We want to stem the tide of ongoing accumulation, and we want to be thoughtful consumers instead of rabid accumulators.

So that's how we arrived at the Cooking Club garage sale and bake sale, with all the proceeds benefiting the Care Center. We sold racks and racks of clothes, all manner of kitchen gear—plates and serving bowls and Crock-Pots. We sold toys and old books and about a zillion pairs of high heels that at some point we felt we needed but clearly are not necessary for this phase of life. We sold tables and chairs and lamps and a ludicrous number of picture frames. We sold stuffed animals and sweatshirts from vacations we went on years and years ago.

We were a little cranky first thing in the morning, but as people started arriving, we got into a groove. The morning hours were a steady stream of people who bought purses and books and DVDs and scarves and high chairs. I was in charge of the bake sale table, which also made me the welcoming committee, right at the edge of the sidewalk as people arrived. We'd made shortbread and pumpkin cream cheese muffins, homemade granola bars and caramel corn, dulce de leche brownies and Gaia cookies, my favorite.

Throughout the day, we'd pop inside every so often to take the cash from our little aprons to the cash box, and at the end of the day we sat around Casey's kitchen with margaritas, dusty and tired, while she counted out every last quarter. We made over a thousand dollars for the Care Center, which feels like an insane amount when you make it mostly in two-dollar increments.

A thousand dollars in the face of a problem like hunger in a city the size of Chicago isn't that much. But it's something. We did something. It's so easy to think that because you can't do something extraordinary, you can't do anything at all. It's easy to decide that if you can't overhaul your entire life in one fell swoop, then you might as well just do nothing. We started where we could, with what we had. I hope it's just the beginning for us. I hope the next time each of us are at Target or Anthropologie, we think a little harder about what that money could buy, about families in our community who need bread and milk and apples more than we need necklaces and sunglasses and cardigans.

That's all we can do: start where we are with what we have. We have so much more than we need, and we spend a lot of our time managing our stuff, picking it up and organizing it and finding places for it. That's not how I want to live. I don't want to stand by, choosing to be ignorant. I want to stand with, choosing to be a part of the solution. I want to be a part of making sure the kids in our town, and in every town, have breakfast, lunch, and dinner, and I want to be clearer about exactly what money can and can't buy.

Gaia Cookies

I've had a longstanding no-baking policy, but one cookie has forced me to break my own rule—the Gaia cookie. The Gaia Café is a fantastic vegetarian hippie restaurant in Grand Rapids, and they're famous for their cookies. One of our favorite things to do when we lived there was to go to Gaia for long, lazy breakfasts of Cuban eggs and cookies and gallons of coffee. My friends in Grand Rapids always bring me cookies from Gaia when they visit, and last Christmas I broke my own rule about not baking because I just had to try to make my all-time favorite cookies.

So when the bake sale idea came around, the other girls all had tons of ideas. They're bakers. They suggested whoopie pies and oatmeal cookies with maple cream frosting, and mini apple pies and cupcakes with buttercream centers and ganache. They suggested cakes and tarts and

Nigella Lawson's caramel croissant bread pudding, which is absolutely amazing.

When it was my turn to tell them what I was going to bring to the bake sale, there was only one option: my cookie, the Gaia cookie. It's one of those cookies that tricks you into thinking it's healthful because it has oats and nuts and dates in it. But it also has sugar and butter and chocolate, so there's really nothing health food about it. It freezes beautifully, and it's the perfect breakfast with a big cup of coffee.

This isn't Gaia's actual recipe, just my best approximation. At Gaia, the cookies are enormous—two or three times the size of an average cookie. I like making them a little smaller so that I feel OK about having two for breakfast.

Ingredients

- ½ pound butter
- 1½ cups brown sugar
- 2 eggs
- 2 tablespoons vanilla
- 1½ cups flour
- 1½ cups oats
- 1 teaspoon baking powder
- 1 teaspoon baking soda
- 1 teaspoon salt
- 1 cup coconut
- 1 cup walnuts, chopped
- 1 cup chocolate chips
- 1 cup chopped dates, raisins, dried cherries, or cranberries, or any combination

Instructions

Preheat oven to 350 degrees.
Cream together butter and brown sugar.
Add eggs and vanilla, and mix well.

Add flour, oats, baking powder, baking soda, salt, and mix well.

Add coconut, walnuts, chocolate chips, and dates or other dried fruit. Mix until combined.

Drop tablespoons of dough onto a cookie sheet lined with parchment paper, 8 per sheet. Refrigerate for a few minutes so the dough doesn't spread out too quickly while baking.

Bake for 14 to 16 minutes or until golden.

MAKES: 2 dozen cookies

last-minute lunch party

Our old friend Shane came to stay with us this spring, and the next morning after church, we had a last-minute lunch party for him and for the friends who wanted to see him while he was in town. Shane is a fascinating, kind, intelligent person—a writer and speaker and activist, a deeply godly person, a Southern boy living in one of the most economically devastated neighborhoods of Philadelphia.

He's been staying with us for years, whenever he comes to town, and he's like a Pied Piper or Kevin Bacon—everyone knows him or wants to know him. People are drawn to him because of his passion and grace, because he speaks like a preacher and poet, and because he lives more simply than anyone I know. I've learned over the years that when Shane comes to our house, there are always last-minute guests, a few extra faces, a rich and lively cast of characters who seem to appear out of nowhere.

Once, when we were living in Grand Rapids, we hosted a party for Shane and a few friends after church. I'd planned on twenty people or so, and I had set out heavy platters of hummus and pita, grilled sausages with spicy mustard, chocolate chip cookies, and sliced melon. So many people turned up that the food was gone instantly, so I kept going back to the kitchen, pillaging the cabinets for anything I could feed them. I peeled a whole crate of clementines and made a huge pile of grilled cheese sandwiches that disappeared from the platter faster than I could keep it filled.

On this particular visit, it would have been easier to go out, of course. It would have been easier to get a head count and make a reservation, and that was our original plan. But I knew there would be more people than we planned. I knew people would turn up at the last minute, excited to see Shane — and with a few extra friends in tow who wanted to meet him. Shane spends so much time traveling, so much time in airports and convention centers, that I knew he'd rather be fed a home-cooked meal than restaurant food. For whatever reason, though, all this only occurred to me at about 11:00 p.m. the night before, and not a moment sooner. We were going to church in the morning, so I had about two hours between church and lunch for twelve people.

Before I went to bed, I defrosted a whole bunch of chicken breasts from the freezer. If I'd had pork tenderloin, I would have used those because they seem just a touch fancier and because it's so easy to grill them, but there is absolutely nothing more versatile in the world than boneless, skinless chicken breasts.

My favorite way to prepare pork tenderloin is in a maple balsamic Dijon glaze, which I thought might work just as well for chicken, and indeed it did. First thing in the morning, after the chicken breasts were thawed, I opened a bottle of beer and located half a jar of a maple Dijon vinaigrette I had made earlier in the week. I dumped the beer over the salted and peppered breasts, then drizzled the vinaigrette thickly over all of it.

The vinaigrette flavors became the guide for the rest of the meal. I tossed mixed greens with the remaining vinaigrette, and also with some croutons I'd made earlier in the week. I'd cooked some maple bacon, and the maple-y bacon grease in the pan seemed too fragrant and yummy to waste, so I threw a few handfuls of cubed bread into it, letting them sizzle and soak in the pan for a while. The maple bacon croutons were a perfect match for the maple Dijon vinaigrette of the salad. Whenever I serve loaves of bread with dinner and there's part of a loaf left over, I slice one part of it into thin slices and another part into cubes and freeze them all so I've always got the bare bones of both crostini and croutons.

For an appetizer, I had located hummus, crumbled feta, and kalamata olives in the fridge, so I layered the three with lots of black pepper. Certainly, plain hummus is fine, especially with a drizzle of olive oil and lots of cracked black pepper, but we eat a lot of hummus in our house, and I get tired of it sometimes. Lately I've been drizzling it with a thick vinaigrette, heavy on the Dijon, or covering it with feta and kalamatas. Since I didn't have crackers, I pulled out half a frozen sliced baguette. I brushed it with garlic oil and salt and pepper and let it toast at 400 degrees on a cookie sheet until it was crispy.

I roasted asparagus with lots of sea salt and pepper, and made a big bowl of quinoa tossed with caramelized onions—something you will always be happy to have on hand—and dried cherries and walnuts. Also, I prepared several more slices of the frozen bread, warmed but not toasted, wrapped in a tea towel, and next to it, a little bowl of butter. When I'm not sure how many people are coming, or how hungry they'll be, I go heavy on the rice or quinoa and also on the bread—those can go a long way, and people walk away satisfied, even after the asparagus and salad are gone.

For dessert, I served little juice glasses of vanilla ice cream and blood orange sorbet. If I'd had enough ripe fruit, a crisp or a crumble would have been perfect, but it was lunch, it was hot, and we ate outside, so ice cream was a great end to the meal, and even though I'm not a huge ice cream eater, I always try to keep one container of french vanilla in the freezer just for occasions like this one.

We crowded around a table in our backyard, old and new faces, strangers and friends. Shane made us laugh and made us think and reminded us of the most important things—faith, courage, daily choices. The meal itself wasn't spectacular by any means, but it didn't need to be. It was simple and it was good and it gave us something to gather around. It filled our bellies and let us laugh and connect and settle into our chairs while the kids played under the table. It did what food is supposed to do: it fed us, in all sorts of big and small ways.

Maple Balsamic Pork Tenderloin

This is my favorite way to serve pork tenderloin, and the marinade and glaze are great on chicken too. What I love about pork tenderloin is that it feels a little bit fancier than chicken, and it's so easy to cook the tenderloins and then slice them and serve them on a big platter as opposed to filling a grill or a pan on the stove with a dozen individual chicken breasts.

Ingredients
- 2 pork tenderloins
- 1 cup maple syrup
- 1 cup balsamic vinegar
- 1 heaping tablespoon Dijon
- ½ cup beer or white wine

Instructions
Whisk together maple syrup, balsamic vinegar, and Dijon.

Add ½ cup of the maple balsamic mixture to the beer or white wine to create a marinade. Save the rest of the maple balsamic mixture to make the glaze.

Several hours before serving, salt and pepper the tenderloins, then pour the marinade over them. Cover tightly and refrigerate.

Just before serving, cook on the grill or on the stove.

On medium-high heat, cook for 3 to 4 minutes on each of the four sides until a meat thermometer reads 145 degrees. Cover with foil and let rest for 10 minutes before slicing. I'm always tempted to rush that part, but all the lovely juices will run out, so if you need to, set the kitchen timer so you're not tempted.

While the pork is cooking and then resting, pour the remaining maple balsamic mixture into a small saucepan and boil gently until reduced by half, about 15 minutes, creating a thick glaze.

After the tenderloin has rested, slice it in diagonal one-inch slices. Pour the glaze over the sliced meat, or put it in a little pitcher and let people pour it on their own slices.

city love

Aaron and I had been ships in the night all week — a wedding, a trip, a recording project. When we reconnected, we were running at the wrong speeds, like when the jump rope is already turning and you can't get your timing right to jump in. We felt a million miles apart, so we did what we've learned to do in this situation over the years: we set down the to-do list, put the kids in the car, and drove the thirty miles to Chicago.

Our first dates were in the city. Our wedding was in the city. Even when we lived in Grand Rapids, we spent anniversaries and special occasions in Chicago. This time we went from store to store, trying on jackets for an upcoming trip, feeding the baby rice teething crackers, and picking up the toys he threw out of the stroller for the thousandth time. We chatted and walked; we held Henry's hand as we crossed the wild intersection in Bucktown, so many streets and lights and walk signals all converging.

We stopped at Big Star for tacos and horchata, chelada and guacamole. Henry had his very first Sprite, and when it came in a tall glass bottle, he looked at us with wide eyes, delighted and half afraid it was a mistake. The restaurant was packed, and the tacos were tiny and delicious, and Mac kicked his legs happily, munching on sweet potatoes.

We learn the hard way over and over that the sweetness of our marriage is directly related to how much time we spend together.

I know some couples who do a little better when they're out of each other's hair, couples who would hate to work together or would drive each other crazy in meetings together or working across from one another at the same table, but for us, time together has always been the medicine we need when things are off.

For our fifth wedding anniversary, we had planned to go to Rome. Our anniversary is in August, but we set aside a week in October, when it would be cooler, when our schedules were freer. We bought guidebooks and made lists of places we wanted to eat. And then I found out I was pregnant and due that exact week we'd set aside. Happily, our trip was put on hold, and we began to plan for Henry instead of Rome.

For that anniversary, instead of a week in Italy, we spent a long weekend in the city, high up in a hotel overlooking Oak Street Beach. I was thirty-six weeks pregnant, so every morning, Aaron brought me a mocha and a maple scone, and then he went on a long run while I lay in bed, crumbs all over my belly, reading baby books. We ordered in Lou Malnati's pizza one night, and another night we sat outside at Iggy's in Bucktown, and I still remember the sharp tang of lemon and goat cheese pasta and the slight chill in the air, summer giving way to fall.

One Thanksgiving, a few years later, right at the last minute, Aaron and Henry and I spent part of the holiday weekend at a cozy hotel in the city. I took a scalding hot bath in the deep tub in our room while Aaron and Henry went out for a walk, and when they came back with hot, spicy Chinese takeout for lunch, we snuggled up on one bed to eat it. Just before Henry's bedtime, we bundled up for my favorite Mexican takeout in the city: thick, fragrant soup; crusty tortas with chorizo; hot chocolate from freshly ground cocoa beans. There, high above the city, we crunched chips and spicy guacamole, thankful beyond words.

For our tenth anniversary, we set aside another week and resurrected our dreams of Italy. You know where this is going, of course, but we didn't, and after so many years, after the miscarriages, after the heartbreaks, we were extra determined to make the trip happen. We had put so many things on hold for the children we couldn't have, and we didn't want to miss such an important anniversary to the maybe-I'll-be-pregnant game, the terrible game we kept playing and losing.

So we set aside the dates, dug out the guidebooks ... and found out I was pregnant, due that week. If we decide to have another baby, maybe the trick is to plan another trip to Italy. We win either way, right?

Italy was off the table, so we talked about Vancouver or San Francisco or New York City. We talked about Austin or Portland or Seattle. But as our anniversary got closer, I was so sick, and only getting sicker. I had stopped traveling for work, and the idea of several hours on a plane sounded terrible. And so once again we found ourselves in Chicago.

This time we stayed in a hotel I had been dreaming about staying at ever since I'd officiated a wedding there the year before. Sometimes when you dream about something for too long, the reality can't live up to your dreams, but that was not the case with this hotel. I was in love with every part of it—the fixtures, the artwork in the lobby, the restaurant, the spa, the super-comfy bed.

I was thirty-five weeks along this time, and it was suffocatingly hot outside, so we mostly stayed in—lots of baths, lots of episodes of *Friday Night Lights* while snuggled up in our big, fancy bed. On the night of our actual anniversary, we had dinner at Le Colonial, a French-Vietnamese restaurant we'd been walking by for years but had somehow never been to. Our friends Rachel and Eric had had their wedding reception there, and when they heard we were eating there, they sent appetizers for us, and the maître d' sent over champagne. We sat at a small table in the middle of the crowded dining room—the good kind of crowded, like we were at a great party. We had shrimp on sugarcanes and fried rice and a coconut macaroon for dessert that blew our minds. We held hands and talked about our wedding, about that night ten years earlier in that same city.

We talked about the funny things and the sweet things, the things that went wrong, the things that were perfect. Before the ceremony we took pictures in Grant Park and at the Art Institute, and as we posed by Buckingham Fountain, a kindergarten class on a field trip came by, and they squealed and pointed as though we were a prince and princess in a fairy tale come to life. The ceremony was officiated by a pastor we love, with lots of beautiful music from dear musician friends.

At the end of the reception, as we ran down the stairs and across the tiled lobby holding hands, our guests tossed handfuls of red rose petals scooped out of heavy silver punch bowls. We waved to everyone and kissed our parents, and then the car sped away, and we looked at each other for just a split second like, "What are we doing?"

Our caterer had packed several foil pans of food for us—crab rangoon, stuffed mushrooms, beef tenderloin with horseradish on toasts, and thick slices of wedding cake—each layer of the chocolate cake had a different filling: lemon, raspberry, hazelnut, espresso. Our hotel room had a window seat overlooking the river, and we sat on the window seat facing each other, the food between us in foil pans. We drank champagne and took bites of mushroom and beef and cake, and we relived every moment of the day.

Ten years later, we both consider the window seat and the cold leftovers to be one of the sweetest moments of our wedding day. You never know while it's happening what will burn in your memory, sacred and profound. It seems like most of the things we try to make profound never are, lost in our insistence and fretting and posing. When we want something to be momentous, it rarely is. Life is disobedient in that way, insisting on surprising us with its magic, stubbornly unwilling to be glittery on command. There are lots of things I don't remember, particularly, about our wedding. It's not that I have no recollection, but rather that it was just another part of the day: cutting the cake, for example, or being announced at the reception as a married couple for the first time. But I do remember that window seat and the glittering lights of the city on the river and the face of my new husband, happy and so handsome.

We had expected to spend our anniversaries in Italy— fountains, pasta, wine, rolling hills, Spanish steps. Instead we spent them in our hometown, in the city we've always loved. It makes every day we spend in the city sweeter for it, because our history is stamped onto these streets and sidewalks, our love story written on this river, this lake, these buildings and street lamps and bridges.

We keep trying to get away, to the other side of the world, to new landscapes and new flavors. We will, at some point. I imagine our current pattern of a baby boy at every big anniversary will not continue, although in some moments I'd like it to. In any case, I love that this city holds so many of our most important memories, whether we planned it that way or not. What it means is that we don't have to go far to find a place that whispers our love songs back to us at every corner. It happened again just this week, on a Tuesday afternoon over tacos and horchata.

better late than never

I promise we intended to dedicate Henry as a baby. Really, we did. Our church dedicates infants rather than baptizing them, reserving baptism for adults. We celebrate dedication as a promise parents make to their children before God and with their community.

Steve and Sarah dedicated Emerson at my parents' cottage. It was a few weeks after my first miscarriage, and a friend suggested it might not be a good idea for me, that it would be safer for me to stay away from something so *baby*, so new life, so directly counter to my life in those days. I understood, certainly, but I found it to be entirely the opposite. Being there helped me to invest myself into what was—a healthy, beautiful baby—instead of continuing to live entirely within what was not—a pregnancy that stopped short, a dream that would never be real.

The sun was setting on the water, and we ate Sarah's stepmom's famous Mexican layered dip (the secret is the homemade refried beans). We took turns holding Henry and Emerson, both squirmy and excited, as we prayed, thanking God for Emerson's life. Later that night after the babies were in bed, we sat around the table together, eating cold refried beans and El Matador chips, drinking red wine. We told funny stories and we also let it be silent sometimes, and as is often the case, I remember so much more about those late, last hours than I do about the official event, when

I was mostly refilling glasses and managing in-laws and squawking babies.

In December of this year, when Mac was teeny, we drove to Kalamazoo because Ryan and Emily asked me to be their daughter Clara's godmother. I'd never been to a Catholic infant baptism, so Clara and I learned the ropes together. It was a sweet morning, the sun slanting through the warm tones of the stained glass in the chapel, Emily's family from Kentucky surrounding us as I held Clara and together we said the words that have been said for generations of babies.

So it seems that all of our friends' children have been meaningfully dedicated or baptized, and somehow, Henry turned five, and it was still on my to-do list. Mom of the year, all five of those years. I was complaining about it, and my cousin Melody jumped in. Her daughter Marley is Henry's age, and they hadn't yet done a dedication.

Melody and I each miscarried three babies in the years between the births of our big kids and our babies. I think there might be more than just flakiness that kept us from dedicating Henry and Marley. I think on some wordless, tender level, we kept thinking if we waited just a little bit longer, we'd have new babies to dedicate. For five years we kept thinking *pretty soon, any time now*, right? Surely? If you haven't lived it, you can't understand how long those years were, and the toll all those months of *pretty soon, any time* took on both our hearts.

But here we were, so deeply and entirely grateful for healthy, wiggly babies growing like weeds. We planned to dedicate our big kids and our babies on a Friday night at my parents' house —the place where we'd had our eighth-grade graduation dinner, Melody's wedding reception, a thousand other milestones and celebrations. Melody and I were born three weeks apart, and we always say we're just like sisters, minus the fighting. Henry and

Marley were born six weeks apart, and our babies, Harper and Mac, six months.

Melody and I are as different as two people can be. She's introverted, organized, routine oriented, cautious; I'm loud, messy, chaotic, chronically overscheduled. She loves meat and potatoes and Classic Coke; I love goat cheese and vinegar and red wine. She wears flip-flops and T-shirts at every possible turn; I consider both leopard and sequins to be neutrals, and I dyed the tips of my hair hot pink this spring.

It makes sense, then, that I'd forget entirely about our plan to dedicate the kids, and that Mel would have to remind me several times. It makes sense that we'd finally set a date, and that I'd fill the week before and the week after with meetings, deadlines, and trips and then ask in desperation if we shouldn't just wait until fall. Gently, Mel told me there was no waiting until fall. The date would stand, and we'd make it happen.

We wanted to keep it as absolutely simple and summery as possible. I'd write the dedication, and we'd make the meal together. We decided on a mini burger bar, Brannon's spicy Caesar salad, Uncle Tim's potato salad, and strawberry cardamom shortcakes for dessert.

We covered my parents' dining room table with butcher paper, and instead of menu cards or signs, we labeled each condiment and topping by writing each bowl's contents right on the paper with thick markers and squiggly arrows. All the standards: lettuce, tomato, ketchup, mustard—both yellow and Dijon—mayonnaise, pickles, sweet relish. Little bowls of caramelized onions, maple bacon, barbecue sauce, and hot banana peppers, and a plate of cheeses: bleu, fresh mozzarella, sharp cheddar. We also papered the kids' table, and they loved drawing on the table so much that they hardly touched their burgers.

The hour leading up to the actual dedication was a rush of

slicing and labeling, and we were eager to get the burgers on the grill, give the kids a chance to play, have the formalities finished. It was wise to make the readings short, with so many kids in attendance, and it was over almost before we knew it. Right at the last second, though, the enormity of what we were doing connected with me, and my tears caught in my throat.

Melody and I and our kids and husbands sat near the fireplace, surrounded by our family and a few friends. Our kids wriggled and babbled while we all read together the words of dedication, and after the reading was finished, my father-in-law prayed a blessing for our kids.

These children, so deeply loved and longed for. This family, so connected and committed to our children. My husband, my cousins, my brother, the house my parents built when I was seven.

One of the themes of my life this season, as much as I hate to admit it, is this: *better late than never*. It's how I begin most of my email replies, what I put in cards on top of birthday gifts and shower gifts that I seem to always be delivering after the fact. Better late than never, unfortunately, is kind of the story of this season of life, when the days feel so short and the months fly by.

I waited five years for that night, and even then, I almost put it off, tired and overly busy. But Melody, my near-sister, my total opposite, was right, as she often is, when she gently but firmly told me we'd keep the date on the calendar, and we'd make it happen no matter what. I'm so thankful she did.

Better late than never, indeed.

Better late than never, in all sorts of ways.

Brannon's Caesar Salad

This isn't a conventional Caesar dressing—it doesn't call for eggs or anchovies, which makes it a great choice for pregnant women and non-anchovy lovers. One friend who tasted it said it's like Caesar and vinaigrette got married and had a baby. Yes, just like that. It's bright and flavorful and a touch spicy, and we ask Brannon to make it at every possible opportunity. This salad provides the perfect occasion to use up frozen bread cubes, and because romaine is hearty and the croutons are homemade and crusty, it's a great option for picnics or open houses.

Ingredients

2 hearts of romaine, washed, dried, and torn into bite-size pieces
2 tablespoons grated Parmesan cheese, plus two more tablespoons for the dressing and the croutons (see below)

Dressing:

1 garlic clove
¼ cup white vinegar
¼ cup olive oil
1 teaspoon Dijon
    A few dashes of Tabasco, to taste
    Juice of half a lemon
1 tablespoon grated Parmesan cheese
1 teaspoon sugar

Croutons:

4 cups bread cubes
1 tablespoon olive oil
1 tablespoon grated Parmesan cheese
    Salt and pepper to taste

Instructions

Preheat the oven to 400 degrees.
On a rimmed baking sheet, toss the frozen bread cubes with olive

oil, salt, pepper, and grated Parmesan. Bake until crispy and golden, 8 to 10 minutes.

Chop garlic clove in food processor, then add remaining ingredients and blend together. Or chop a garlic clove, drop it into the bottom of an old pickle jar or jelly jar, add everything else, and shake like crazy.

Toss romaine lettuce with Parmesan croutons, grated Parmesan, and dressing.

SERVES: 6 to 8

swimsuit, ready or not

I'm a summer girl. Summer is my favorite season. Summer is long days, going barefoot, sunsets on the lake. It's fireworks and lazy mornings and no school and no routine. It's flip-flops and sundresses and tan shoulders and ponytails. It's farmers markets and Long Island Iced Teas and fried shrimp in a basket and boating and swimming and sandy toes and pink noses. Summer food is my favorite food—berries and corn and peaches and tomatoes and everything cooked on the grill.

There is, however, one tiny thing I don't like about summer: I'm not wild about swimsuits. It's been years since I've had a summer where I wasn't pregnant or nursing or post-baby-puffy. Even before that, I was never a swimwear model candidate. On my best days, I can look decent in jeans, but swimsuits don't do me any favors, and as luck would have it, I spend a good portion of the summer up at the lake, wearing a swimsuit from morning till night. I love being at the lake, of course, but at the beginning of every summer, I have to do a little internal business, organizing my thoughts and feelings and phobias, getting myself ready to let everyone I know see me in a piece of clothing that could fit into a sandwich bag.

But as my friend Sara always reminds me, no one's actually thinking about me as often as I think they are. Probably my friends are not actually counting the days till summer to see if I've finally turned into a supermodel. Probably they're thinking about their own lives or current events or any number of things that have nothing to do with my chins.

That's what shame does, though. It whispers to us that everyone is as obsessed with our failings as we are. It insists that there is, in fact, a watchdog group devoted completely to my weight or her wrinkles or his shrinking bank account. Shame tricks us into believing there's a cable channel that runs video footage of us in our underpants twenty-four hours a day, and that all the people we respect have seen it. Shame tells us that we're wrong for having the audacity to be happy when we're so clearly terrible. Shame wants us to be deeply apologetic for just daring to exist.

But I've been watching that footage on a loop for too long. I've been my own watchdog group for decades. I want to do something risky. I want to dare to exist and, more than that, to live audaciously, in all my imperfect, lumpy, scarred glory, because the alternative is letting shame win.

So here we are again, my favorite time of year, summer at the lake, and the idea of someone—anyone!—seeing me in my swimsuit makes me feel a little anxious. I want to find any and every excuse to stay covered, stay inside, stay invisible.

But if I do that, I'll miss the best parts of summer. I'll miss the beach. I'll miss the breathtaking plunges off the back of the boat into really, really cold water. I'll miss paddleboarding and boogie boarding. I'll miss watching Mac float around, kicking his legs with a huge smile on his little face, and I'll miss racing Henry in the lake from there to there a thousand times in a row.

So this is what I'm going to do: I'm going to swim. I'm going to paddleboard. I'm going to make sand castles and make-believe and make memories with my kids. I'm going to cannonball into the icy lake water. I'm going to live in the body God made me, not because it's perfect but because it's mine. And I'm going to be thankful for health and for the ability to run and move and dance and swim.

And this is what I'm not going to do: I'm not going to hide. I'm not going to bow out of things I love to do because I'm afraid people won't love me when they see my underbutt.

This is the promise I'm making: this summer, I'm not going to be ashamed of my body. Or at the very least, I'm not going to let a lifetime of shame about my body get in the way of living in a rich, wild, grateful, wide-open way.

I'm not going to give in to the cultural pressure that says women's bodies are only beautiful when they're very, very small. I'm going to take up every inch of space I need. I'm going to practice believing that I am more than my body, that I am more than my hips, that I am more than my stretch-marked stomach. I'm going to allow my shoulders to feel the sun, and even (gasp!) my thighs, instead of making sure I'm always, always safely covered and out of your view.

I'm not going to bow to the voice inside my head that says I should be ashamed of myself for being so unruly and wild. I'm not going to develop a relationship with my cover-up that borders on obsessive. This summer, I'm not going to hide.

This is my promise to you, and also my invitation.

Repeat after me: *swimsuit, ready or not, here I come.*

Farmers Market Potato Salad

This salad came about exactly as the name suggests: at the farmers market. One of my favorite stalls always has beautiful stacks of radishes and baskets of potatoes, and every time I go to the market, I'm seduced by those radishes. I buy herbs and green beans and tomatoes, peaches and raspberries and flowers, and then our kitchen looks like a veritable garden for a few days, in the best possible way, and I have to hurry up and use everything before the next market day.

I love potato salad. I like the kind with mayonnaise and the kind with mustard and lots of pickles. I like celery and big hunks of red potatoes, or tiny bits of peeled potatoes with hard-boiled eggs. I like them all, but this is my favorite. Ina Garten's french potato salad is the starting point for this recipe, but I'm too lazy in the summertime to toss the potatoes with the stock and wine, so instead I toss them with the vinaigrette and throw in almost any summer vegetable I can find.

An easy way to hard-boil eggs: put the eggs in a pan and completely cover them with cold water. Bring the water to a rolling boil on high heat, and then turn the heat off and put the cover on the pan. Leave it covered, off heat, for 12 minutes, then remove the eggs from the water with a slotted spoon and put them in a bowl of cold water so they stop cooking.

A note on blanching the green beans: put a pot of water on the stove and let it come to a boil while you snap the ends off the beans. Fill a bowl with ice, and when the water on the stove boils, throw the green beans in for two minutes. Then lift them out with a slotted spoon and put them in the ice water for two minutes, then on a towel to dry. Blanching preserves the bright green color and makes them crunchy. If you want to be really efficient, I bet you could blanch your beans in with the potatoes while they're boiling away. You'd be a genius, I think.

Ingredients

2 pounds red and gold potatoes
1 cup pitted kalamata olives, halved
1 cup grape tomatoes, halved

4 hard-boiled eggs, quartered

1 cup radishes, thinly sliced

1 cup green beans, ends snapped, blanched, and cut into bite-size pieces

2 tablespoons fresh basil

2 tablespoons fresh dill

Vinaigrette:

1 tablespoon Dijon

½ cup balsamic vinegar

1 cup olive oil

Salt and pepper to taste

Instructions

Cut red and gold potatoes into bite-size chunks, then boil in salted water till fork tender. While the potatoes are boiling, make the vinaigrette, and reserve a few tablespoons for tossing right before serving.

Drain the potatoes, then toss them with dressing while they're still hot so it all soaks in. I do this early in the day, or the day before, for extra flavor soaking.

Add olives, grape tomatoes, eggs, radishes, and green beans, and toss together. Then add lots of fresh basil and dill, salt and pepper, and the reserved dressing. I like this best at room temperature instead of refrigerated, so it's perfect for a summer dinner party. You can make it early in the day, and that's one less thing to do right before your guests arrive.

SERVES: 8

the mayor of the river

My brother, Todd, and I are both summer babies—his birthday in July, and mine in August—so when I think about our birthdays, I always think about South Haven and about the lake. Last year, we planned to have dinner at the cottage for his birthday. It stormed on and off all week, dark rolling storms with cracks of thunder and low skies. We lost power several times, and trees fell all over town. The day of his birthday broke just the same, gray and windy, but before dinner the sun came out, and instead of dinner inside, we took everything out onto the boat at the last minute. We went swimming off the back of the boat and sang happy birthday to him in wet swimsuits, reveling in the unexpected sunshine after a week of wind and clouds.

We call Todd the mayor of the river—he spends more time on boats than ten average boaters put together, and he knows absolutely everyone in town. He sails and paddleboards and jet-skis, and he spends every weekend year-round in this tiny lakeshore town. He lives in Chicago, working long crazy hours in finance, but every Friday afternoon he heads straight for the lake, and by sunset he resumes his post as the mayor of the river.

As a part of his birthday gift this year, my mom put together a slide show of his sailing trip around the world, so after dinner we looked through hundreds of images of remote anchorages and unfamiliar landscapes, sunsets over the water and green mountains rising out of rough navy seas. His sailing trip began and ended in South Haven. They left early on the morning of Henry's first birthday and arrived back in this same harbor the day after Mother's Day almost two years later, the very best Mother's Day gift my mom could have asked for.

People always asked my mom if she was scared, having him so far away on such a small boat, and she always answered the same way. She told them that one of the chief aspects of mothering is prayer, and that she had learned very early with a son like Todd — a son who loves to sail and snowboard and ride dirt bikes and drive race cars and build motorcycles — that prayer was the only thing that would keep her sane.

After being gone for almost two years, one clear spring Monday, Todd sailed back home, back down the river, into the harbor where both my grandpas had sailed decades before, where my dad learned to sail, and where he taught his son, my brother. My mother's prayers for a safe return were answered, and our friends and family packed the little yacht club to celebrate his return and his safe passage around the world.

This river, this yacht club, this town holds a million childhood memories for me, and now we're making a million more with our boys and our friends. Both boys have learned to walk in South Haven. Five summers ago, Henry learned to walk in the blue house we rent every summer, and earlier this month, Mac took his very first step at the park down the street, the lake sparkling in the evening sun, the kids' squawks and screams from the playground drifting across a field down to the beach.

But if you stay anywhere long enough, it will start to accumulate some shadows. And those shadows make it no less beautiful. It makes it something like home. It anchors you there in ways that a steady diet of pleasantness never will. I remember sitting on the steps of the blue house when a friend told me her marriage was ending. One year, when a friend and her kids arrived, while our kids yelped and hugged, my friend cried with me on the porch, caught off guard by the memory of announcing her pregnancy the year before, only to have it end in miscarriage weeks later.

One summer I sat with a friend while she sobbed about a breakup, and on that same porch, I had one of the hardest conversations of my life with another friend. We looked out at the street, not at each other, sitting shoulder to shoulder as I told her that I thought her drinking had gone too far, and that something big had to change. Life unfolding, rich and broken and beautiful and heartbreaking, in that town, under those trees, along that stretch of beach, on that porch. Last summer, two families we love had babies while we were there, so we celebrated Clara Marine and Deacon Carter, summer babies, just like my brother and me.

This year, for Todd's birthday, my parents planned to host dinner, but I wanted to cook. I took the boys down to their cottage early in the afternoon. My parents were thrilled to have a few hours with the boys, and I was aching to cook—aching, in fact, to be alone and to do something with my hands, something creative and productive, something real.

We'd had friends visiting all week—trips to Saugatuck on the boat, burgers with sweet potato fries at the Mermaid, cans of Blue Moon and wood-fired pizzas, scoops of Sherman's chocolate malt supreme ice cream, and walks on the pier to watch the sunset.

Every year I say we're going to keep it low-key and have almost no houseguests, and then every year we fill up the house like we're running a bed-and-breakfast, and what seems like a good idea on the calendar a few months out becomes a mad dash for groceries and toilet paper between groups of visitors. I'm not going to complain about ice cream and a walk on the pier almost every night with a different group, but it does make it tricky to get enough sleep or get any work done at all.

I had been so frustrated with the writing I was trying to finish, and I loved having friends in town, but I wasn't sleeping nearly enough, and was hardly reading at all. I felt far from myself, and I raced through the grocery store, so excited to spread out all over a quiet kitchen, to make a mess.

As the grill heated, I shucked eighteen ears of corn, way more than enough for the recipe. I got carried away because there's something so quintessentially summery about shucking corn on a porch, and besides, leftovers are such a great thing to have on busy summer days. I soaked the ears for a few minutes, then grilled them on high heat until they were charred and black in some spots and bright yellow in others. While the ears cooled, I chopped scallions and celery and green apples for turkey burgers, and then marinated chunks of watermelon in lime juice for the watermelon feta salad. I cut the corn off the cobs and mixed in mayonnaise, Cotija cheese, lime juice, cilantro, and cayenne—my version of traditional Mexican-grilled street corn. I chopped parsley for the burgers and then made a lime vinaigrette for the salad.

After the burgers were formed and wrapped and chilling, I made a blueberry crisp, oats and pecans scattered all over the counter, piles of ears of corn in one corner and watermelon rinds in another. I worked silently, let phone calls go to voice mail, ignored my to-do list. I didn't do laundry. I didn't catch up on emails. For what seemed like the first time in a long time, I wasn't multitasking. I wasn't watching the baby while getting Henry a bowl of cereal, or trying to write a few more sentences before Mac woke up from his nap. I wasn't late for anything, wasn't rushing anywhere, wasn't packing or unpacking a cooler or a tote bag or a suitcase or a diaper bag.

I was only there, and I was the only one there.

All the chopping and measuring and stirring felt like a sacred act, and I found myself praying for my brother as I cooked, thinking about his life, his year to come. I prayed for every part of his life —for his health and safety, for his friendships, for his dreams and fears. I prayed for what the year might hold, and I thanked God for him, for the gift that it is to be his sister.

Because Todd is my only sibling, and I am his, there's something completely singular about our relationship. There's no one on earth who has shared our history, no one on earth who can see the world from the corner that we alone inhabit. As children, we played on the beach together for hundreds of hours. Our friends were back at home playing video games and going to sports camps, but he and I, he and I, were always at the lake, each other's best playmate by default.

Now we are grown. And he is still one of my best friends, first phone calls, closest companions. There is a whole world, a whole history between us that no one else knows, that no one else understands, and there are times when my brother and I catch eyes in a room, across the dinner table, or across the yacht club, understanding each other perfectly, wordlessly. What a gift it is to share this town, this history, this family, this corner of the world with someone like him.

Happy birthday, little brother.

Happy birthday—to the mayor of the river.

Mar-a-Lago Turkey Burgers

Adapted from O, The Oprah Magazine.

Apparently when Oprah visited Donald Trump at his famous Palm Beach house, Mar-a-Lago, his chef served these amazing turkey burgers. She asked for the recipe because they were the best turkey burgers she'd ever had. And I completely agree with her. I love these burgers.

This ingredient list might put you off, both because it's a little kooky and because it requires a pretty serious amount of chopping. Do not be deterred. Seriously. Settle in for a nice meditative chopping session, or enlist some pals and pass out the apples, the celery, the scallions—or feel free to use your food processor for chopping.

This isn't a recipe you want to start a half hour before your friends come over for a barbecue. Make them the night before, and while you're at it, make a double batch and freeze half. The burgers take a while to assemble, and then they do need to chill for a while. But once they're assembled and chilling, you're going to be so happy about your dinner. I promise.

The secret ingredient in these burgers is mango chutney—I'm a huge mango chutney fan. One of my favorite predinner snacks is crackers with sharp white cheddar and mango chutney, and my favorite way to make chicken salad is by mixing diced cooked chicken with cream cheese, mango chutney, and a little curry powder. Trader Joe's makes a good mango chutney, and most grocery stores carry it in the international/ ethnic aisle in the Indian food section—sometimes it's called Major Grey's Chutney. When you find it, stock up—get one jar for this recipe, another for chicken salad, and one for serving with cheese and crackers.

I like these burgers on whole wheat buns, with a slice of Vermont white cheddar and a little bit of special sauce (recipe below).

Ingredients

¼ cup scallions, thinly sliced
½ cup celery, finely chopped
3 Granny Smith apples, peeled and diced

Olive oil

4 pounds ground turkey breast

1 tablespoon salt

1 tablespoon black pepper

2 teaspoons Tabasco

Juice of 1 lemon

½ bunch parsley, finely chopped

¼ cup mango chutney

Special sauce:

½ cup mango chutney

½ cup mayonnaise

½ cup ketchup

2 dashes Tabasco, or to taste

Instructions

Sauté the scallions, celery, and apples in olive oil until tender. Let cool.

While the mixture is cooling, make the special sauce. Mix chutney, mayonnaise, ketchup, and Tabasco. Adjust for heat and then refrigerate until serving time.

Place the ground turkey in a large mixing bowl. Add sautéed items and the remaining ingredients. Shape into 12 burgers. Refrigerate for 2 hours.

Place on a preheated, lightly oiled grill set to medium-high heat. Grill each side for 7 minutes until meat is thoroughly cooked. Let sit for 5 minutes.

MAKES: 12 burgers

pont neuf

I started learning French when I was seven, and went to Paris for the first time when I was twelve. My love for that city began when I was a child, and it hasn't faded yet.

I visited Paris in junior high and in high school, and on a free weekend during my college semester in England, six of us decided to take the Eurostar over to Paris and find a place to stay when we arrived. Actually, five of us, because Kirsten heard our plan and decided we were crazy, so she booked herself a flight and a hotel on Île Saint-Louis and told us she'd see us there.

When the five of us arrived at Gare du Nord, the main train station in Paris, very late at night, a woman approached us. She told us she was Canadian and that she rented out rooms in her apartment in a good neighborhood to young travelers. This seemed legitimate to us, for no reason at all, so we followed her into the night, and into her apartment, the walls of which were hung, floor to ceiling, with medieval weapons. Red flag upon red flag.

Against all odds, she did not at any point murder any of us with her multiple decorative weapons, and each morning she came into our rooms with eggs and baguettes. The moral of this story is that we were horribly young and trusting, and it worked out well, which led us to believe we could continue being young and trusting. And we did.

But that was sixteen years ago, and this time around I was not traveling with a backpack and several other twenty-year-olds. I was traveling with a baby, a five-year-old, my husband, my mother-in-law, two rolling suitcases, and two strollers. A sleek and nimble operation, obviously.

We were coming from London, and we didn't totally think through how tired we'd be after a few days of work outside London and a few busy sightseeing days in London, strollering around the city, marching up and down the tube stations over and over. We took the Eurostar and arrived at Gare du Nord late at night once again, tired and covered with Mac's chewed-up croissant paste. We learned in London that Mac loved croissants, and the love affair continued, naturally, in Paris.

It took us a little while to get our act together at Gare du Nord —to switch from train station to Metro station, find the right Metro, take Henry to the bathroom. *Wait! You need euros for the bathroom. I'll get euros. You take Henry to the bathroom.*

I was in line for Metro tickets when I heard my mother-in-law yell. Aaron was chasing someone up the escalator, and that person was carrying Diane's bag. He relinquished it easily, and then he was absorbed into a yelling, pointing little mob and led away. I told the man at the ticket counter what had happened, panicky and stumbling over my rusty French, and he said, with absolutely no interest at all, "Bienvenue à Paris, madame." *Welcome to Paris, ma'am.*

Our adrenaline was pumping and we were wound up and everyone looked sinister, a terrible introduction to such a beautiful city. When we finally did get to our Metro stop, the walk to our hotel felt harrowing and chaotic until we realized that all the sirens were ambulances going to a nearby hospital, not police cars.

The hotel had gotten our reservation wrong, and the extra room for my mother-in-law was not available. But it was close to midnight, very hot, and we were no longer in the mood to make decisions. The five of us crammed into a closet-sized room on the fifth floor, and we spread out all our snacks on the narrow desk, extemporizing dinner. Diane had granola bars and fruit snacks. I had toffee and Cadbury Dairy Milk bars and some mixed nuts, and while we made Henry a little bed on the floor, Aaron went out for bottled water.

He came back with water, and with a paper cup of champagne for me. All the stores were closed, but an Indian restaurant was still open, and he begged the owners for champagne for his wife, who had just arrived in her favorite city. The husband shook his head, but the wife relented, and that paper cup of champagne was about the sweetest thing Aaron ever gave me.

When he returned, we realized that while our hotel room was absolutely tiny and very hot, it had a stunning view of the Eiffel Tower, so we took turns squeezing onto the balcony and toasting with that paper cup of champagne.

That's Paris. That's the magic of that city. Someone tries to steal your bag. Everyone on the Metro glares at your multiple suitcases and strollers. The hotel loses your reservation and you end up walking up five flights of stairs and having mixed nuts for dinner and cramming three adults and two kids into a hotel room the size of a compact car. And then you stand on a narrow balcony with your hands on a wrought iron railing and you point out the Eiffel Tower, sparkling and glowing, to your fascinated, exhausted five-year-old, and all is forgiven.

The next morning, Aaron and I brought back coffee and breakfast—huge wedges of a buttery berry crumble, and, of course, a croissant for Mac. Later that day we changed hotels, and we found the new one to be as charming and lovely as the other one was stuffy and small, and our new neighborhood seemed sweet and inviting immediately.

We went to the Eiffel Tower, took a bateau mouche to Notre Dame. We walked through the silent cathedral with hundreds of other people, a slow-moving, whispering procession. Whenever I'm in a Catholic church, I light a candle and say a prayer, and that afternoon at the Notre Dame, the cathedral named for Mary, I prayed for the many women in my life who are aching to be mothers. I prayed for babies upon babies for those women.

Henry was absolutely enamored with the cathedral, and begged me to ask someone who worked there about the hunchback. I'm sorry to say I tried to trick him and ask an American college-aged girl who was standing next to us at one point, but he saw right through that, and he wanted his answer from an actual employee. So as we exited the cathedral, I found a group of men who worked there, and they assured him it was nothing more than a legend—that there was no "monster" in this beautiful church.

We walked home along Boulevard St Germain, and we stopped for gelato at Amorino, where they sculpt the gelato into the shape of rose petals so your cone looks like a perfect flower.

Diane stayed with the boys in the evenings so Aaron and I could go out for dinner, and Brannon told me there was only one restaurant we absolutely had to go to: Le Relais de l'Entrecôte. We were delighted to find it was right in our neighborhood, and we sat outside on Boulevard du Montparnasse and ate steak frites that were so good we hardly talked to each other, mouths full and happy.

After dinner we wandered into the Jardin du Luxembourg. Because it wasn't on our "must-visit" list, because we weren't strolling to it with the kids and snacks, one more thing to see on our blitz of Paris, it felt like a secret garden, a discovery, a treat.

Again, that Paris charm. We walked slowly, lazily. We held hands and laughed about how Paris has to be the only city in the world where you actually can't sit on the grass in a public park. We watched people gathering around the edges of the pond in small groupings, drinking wine and eating sandwiches on ficelles, so quintessentially Parisian that it felt like a film set.

We bought huge meringues, raspberry-flavored and the size of baseball gloves, one for Aaron and one to take back to his mother, and then we walked back to the hotel in the fading light, feeling lucky and full.

The next day we went to the Place de la Concorde and the Jardin des Tuileries. We walked past Notre Dame again, and across the small footbridge to Île Saint-Louis. We had ice cream at Berthillon and then made our way home along Boulevard St Germain, shaded by the huge trees.

Aaron and I had grand plans for our last night—Montmartre and Sacré-Cœur, maybe, or a dinner cruise along the Seine. But the day was long and our flight was early the next morning. We decided to pick up the components of a picnic dinner from Au Bon Marché and eat on the banks of the Seine—another quintessentially Parisian night.

We held hands as we walked, and we spread a little blanket on the cobblestones on the riverbank just across from Notre Dame. We ate bread and cheese and drank rosé. We people-watched and looked up at the deepening yellow light on the famous cathedral. Once again, the charm of Paris—like nothing else in the world.

After dinner I asked Aaron if we could walk to the Pont Neuf, just to stand on it for a minute, just to be there, right there, right at that time of day. When I went to Paris for the first time, more than twenty years ago, I stayed near the Pont Neuf, and I remember with perfect clarity what it felt like to stand on that beautiful bridge. They say the color of the air in Paris is the exact color of champagne, and I remember standing on that bridge at that golden hour when the sun had dipped lower than the rooftops in the distance but the sky was still full of light, glowing and golden.

Or maybe I didn't actually remember it. That's what I was afraid of. That the Paris of my imagination didn't exist, that it was just that—imagination. I'd been reading about this city all my life, watching movies, looking at photographs. Paris was the city of my imagination, my childhood dreams. Along the way, I started to wonder if it was only in my imagination, if my mind held it as this uniquely beautiful place, but then when I went back, no longer a child, I would find that it was just another city, just another busy, crowded sprawl.

And then we stood on the Pont Neuf that hot June night, and to my surprise, I cried. Because the Paris of my imagination was absolutely real, absolutely more beautiful, even, than my mind and heart remembered it. We stood holding hands on that breathtaking bridge, looking down the river at the Eiffel Tower and up the river at Notre Dame, and I felt blessed and lucky deep in my bones, so thankful that this extraordinary place was indeed real, and that even more, I got to be a part of it, even if just for a few days.

That's how it felt, like we were a part of something lovely and otherworldly, not like we went to a place but like we were a part of a thing—a rich and gorgeous thing, a happening, a moment in time that we'd keep with us all our lives, like wearing a locket around your neck. I had feared the Paris I loved as a little girl existed only in my little-girl imagination. What a gift to find it real, a living and breathing place; what a gift to stand on that bridge all these years later.

Now we are home, our days marked by grocery shopping and laundry, bedtime and naptime, diapers and baths and helping Henry learn to read. But every once in a while, I find my mind turning to Paris, and my heart swells just for a second, because it's real, because we stood on that bridge and I fell under its spell all over again.

Simplest Dark Chocolate Mousse

Adapted from Bon Appetit

There is nothing more French, of course, than chocolate mousse, but you already know I'm a terrible baker, and the idea of tempering eggs is more than I can manage. This mousse, then, is the ultimate cheater mousse since it has only three ingredients, since it contains no eggs and no butter, and since there's no cooking, actually, aside from melting together the cream, chocolate, and honey. Even I can handle that. It does require you to whisk until your arm practically falls off, but I feel like that's good exercise, right? And you can always use an electric mixer if you'd rather.

You can serve the mousse in individual ramekins or footed glasses, but I like to serve it in juice glasses, casual and sweet, with a bowl of raspberries.

Ingredients

2 cups (1 pint) chilled heavy cream, divided
1½ cups (12 ounces) dark chocolate chips
¼ cup honey

Instructions

Stir ¾ cup cream, chocolate, and honey in saucepan over low heat until smooth. Cool for a few minutes, stirring occasionally.

In a separate bowl, beat ¾ cup cream to soft peaks. Fold cream into chocolate mixture in 2 additions.

Divide mousse among 6 glasses or ramekins. Refrigerate until set, about 2 hours.

Whisk the remaining ½ cup cream to firm peaks. Spoon a little bit of cream on top of each mousse. Top with a couple berries, or just serve the fruit alongside.

SERVES: 6

take this bread

I haven't baked bread since college, when I went through a brief but intense baguette phase, baking pan after pan of slim loaves, wrapping them in dish towels while they were still hot, cradling them like babies in the crook of my arm, arriving at friends' houses and neighbors' homes with still-warm, crusty, golden bread.

This fall, something in me felt compelled to start again. All this talk of bread and wine made me want to knead, bake, break open—steam escaping, crust cracking. It's fall, which brings out a little melancholy, I think. And it's a season of great change in our home: our boys are turning from baby to toddler and little boy to big. Mac's first birthday is this month, and Henry just started kindergarten. One bright Monday morning a few weeks ago, he put on his Superman backpack and climbed up the big stairs of a yellow school bus, and that was that: our boy is big.

Maybe it was the change in the air, or the changes under our roof, maybe it was the nature of writing—so much activity in the mind and the heart and the fingers, and sometimes you have to close the computer and live in the world again: flour, salt, water, roaring hot oven, butter melting into the steaming crags.

I began to bake bread, loaf after loaf, flour in my hair and cuticles, my well-loved red dutch oven put to work for the rising, and the sweet Cath Kidston tea towels we brought home from London this summer pressed into service over the rising dough.

When the first loaf came out of the oven, hot and crusty, the whole house smelling like heaven, I almost cried. It was the strangest thing. I make plenty of things that are much more difficult, but maybe that's the point. Maybe it's the simplicity that got me, not the difficulty.

That first loaf did not seem to be going well—the rising seemed halfhearted, and I had myself steeled for a failure. But when I opened the oven, there it was, a gorgeous, crusty, piping-hot loaf that I showed off, bursting with pride, to my mother and my mother-in-law. I was like a child with a project—*I made this! I made it from flour and water! All by myself!*

It felt like an epiphany, a discovery. I wanted to tell everyone I know. I started making loaf after loaf, every chance I got. I ate it with butter and jam, with cheddar and Dijon, with goat cheese and honey, and mostly just plain, fresh from the oven, so hot I burned both my fingers and my tongue and kept eating anyway.

I've been a self-professed non-baker for a long time, but that's all over now. The signs, really, have been pointing that way for some time. I told myself that the toffee and the mousse aren't really baking—more like melting and whipping. But now my once-a-year-only-at-Christmas Gaia cookies have started appearing in all seasons, the breakfast cookies have become a staple, and Nigella's brownies are making frequent after-dinner appearances. And then my over-the-top summer-of-blueberry-crisp forced me out into the open: I'm baking, people, and not occasionally. But this is it: this bread is the final step. This bread has made me a baker.

Baking bread feels so deeply right, on so many levels, like going back to the beginning. I've been making risotto and reducing balsamic on the stove, caramelizing onions and whipping cream for mousse, dredging chicken for a curry and shucking corn to be grilled. But before all that, under all that, at the beginning:

there was bread. The element, itself, the most basic building block: bread.

While I measured and kneaded, while the dough rose, while the oven reached a screaming 450, I let my mind wander: Why does it matter? Why does food matter? Why does the table matter?

Food matters because it's one of the things that forces us to live in this world—this tactile, physical, messy, and beautiful world—no matter how hard we try to escape into our minds and our ideals. Food is a reminder of our humanity, our fragility, our createdness. Try to think yourself through starvation. Try to command yourself not to be hungry, using your own sheer will. It will work for a while, maybe, but at some point you'll find yourself —no matter how high-minded or iron-willed—face-to-face with your own hunger, and with that hunger, your own humanity.

The sacraments are tangible ways to represent intangible ideas: new life becomes something we can feel and smell and see when we baptize in water. The idea of a Savior, of a sacrifice, of body and blood so many centuries ago, fills our senses and invades our present when our fingers break bread and our mouths fill with wine.

We don't experience this connection, this remembering, this intimate memory and celebration of Christ, only at the altar. We experience it, or at least we could, every time the bread and wine are present—essentially, every time we are fed. During that last meal, that last gathering of dear friends and disciples, Jesus was inviting us to gather around a table and remember, in church buildings and outside of them, during the sacrament of Communion and outside of it.

When you offer peace instead of division, when you offer faith instead of fear, when you offer someone a place at your table instead of keeping them out because they're different or messy or wrong somehow, you represent the heart of Christ.

We tend to believe that what we've done is too bad—that our sins and mistakes are beyond repair, and our faults and failures too deep and ugly. That's what shame tells us. But if we take a chance and come to the table, and if when we are there we are treated with respect and esteem and kindness, then that voice of shame recedes, just for a little while, enough to let the voice of truth, of hope, of Christ himself, get planted a little deeper and a little deeper each time. The table becomes the hospital bed, the place of healing. It becomes the place of relearning and reeducating, the place where value and love are communicated.

When the table is full, heavy with platters, wine glasses scattered, napkins twisted and crumpled, forks askew, dessert plates scattered with crumbs and icing, candles burning down low—it's in those moments that I feel a deep sense of God's presence and happiness. I feel honored to create a place around my table, a place for laughing and crying, for being seen and heard, for telling stories and creating memories.

I do sometimes feel a sense of God's presence when I write, or when I listen, or when I read the Bible. I often feel that sacred flickering when I hold my baby, or when I kiss Henry's eyelids when he's sleeping. I feel it when I look across the lake or when I see the ocean. But more than anything, I feel it at the table.

Body of Christ, broken for you. Blood of Christ, shed for you. "Every time you eat the bread and drink the wine," Jesus says, "remember me." Communion is connection, remembrance.

My friend Shane says the genius of Communion, of bread and wine, is that bread is the food of the poor and wine the drink of the privileged, and that every time we see those two together, we are reminded of what we share instead of what divides us.

In our tradition, we take Communion as a part of the church service every month or so. We pass a plate of bread, and another with tiny cups of wine—juice, actually. The taste of grape juice always reminds me of church, because until I had children, that was the only time I ever encountered it. We also celebrate Communion in less formal places—at a camp, or on a retreat. It isn't terribly uncommon to take Communion together in a makeshift way, in a home or a backyard or on a beach, one person reading the Scripture, another passing the bread and wine around a circle of friends, a small group, or a team that serves together.

I believe the bread and wine is for all of us, for every person, an invitation to believe, a hand extended from divine to human. I believe it's to be torn and handled, gulped. I believe that we can practice the sacrament of Communion anywhere at all, that a forest clearing can become a church and any one of us a priest as we bless the bread and the wine.

And I believe that Jesus asked for us to remember him during the breaking of the bread and the drinking of the wine every time, every meal, every day—no matter where we are, who we are, what we've done.

If we only practice remembrance every time we take Communion at church, we miss three opportunities a day to remember. What a travesty! Eugene Peterson says that "to eyes that see, every bush is a burning bush." Yes, that, exactly. To those of us who believe that all of life is sacred, every crumb of bread and sip of wine is a Eucharist, a remembrance, a call to awareness of holiness right where we are.

I want all of the holiness of the Eucharist to spill out beyond the church walls, out of the hands of priests and into the regular streets and sidewalks, into the hands of regular, grubby people like you and me, onto our tables, in our kitchens and dining rooms and backyards.

Holiness abounds, should we choose to look for it. The whisper and drumbeat of God's Spirit are all around us, should we choose to listen for them. The building blocks of the most common meal —the bread and the wine—are reminders to us: "He's here! God is here, and he's good." Every time we eat, every time we gather, every time the table is filled: *He's here. He's here, and he is good.*

Sullivan Street Bread

Ingredients and instructions by Jim Lahey,
owner of Sullivan Street Bakery.

I've been hearing about this recipe for years, but my fear of yeast has kept me away. And then all at once, on a cool fall day, I plunged in, and I have to tell you, this is incredible bread, and incredibly easy.

A few notes: I use my beloved, battered, scratched Le Creuset dutch oven, and it works perfectly. Also, every time I make it, I hope that this time it's going to rise into a huge, puffy, impressive sphere, and really, it never does. Mine never doubles the way the recipe says it will. This is nerve-racking every time, and then the bread is delicious every time. Like life, right? We freak out, generally, for nothing. That's how this bread is. It makes me nervous and makes me certain I've failed, and then it delights me with that crusty, crackling, gorgeous loaf. Bread baking is an emotional roller coaster. Hold on tight.

Also, I use cornmeal to dust it because I like the gritty yellowness, and I'm pretty generous with it, especially on the tea towel so it doesn't get all sticky.

A few more things: the recipe instructs you to let the dough rest for 12 hours—feel free to leave it longer than that, but not shorter. At our house, I bake it at 450 degrees for 45 minutes, and that's perfect. You might find that 500 works better for you, or that in your oven you need the whole hour, but my recommendation is that you start with 450 and 45 minutes.

And then call me and yell and dance around your kitchen, because you have cracked the code, found the grail, unlocked the key: you have made bread.

Ingredients

   3 cups all-purpose flour
  ¼ teaspoon yeast
1¼ teaspoons salt
1½ cups water
     Olive oil (about one tablespoon, for coating)
     Extra flour, wheat bran, or cornmeal (about 2 tablespoons, for dusting)

Equipment:

     2 medium mixing bowls
     6- to 8-quart pot with lid (Pyrex glass, Le Creuset cast iron, or ceramic)
     Wooden spoon
     Plastic wrap
     2 or 3 cotton dish towels (not terry cloth)

Instructions

Mix all of the dry ingredients in a medium bowl. Add water and incorporate with a wooden spoon or spatula for 30 seconds to 1 minute.

Lightly coat the inside of a second medium bowl with olive oil and place the dough in the bowl. Cover the bowl with plastic wrap and let the dough rest 12 hours at room temperature (approximately 65 to 72 degrees).

After 12 (or more) hours, remove the dough from the bowl and fold once or twice. Let the dough rest 15 minutes in the bowl or on the work surface.

Next, shape the dough into a ball. Generously coat a cotton towel with flour, wheat bran, or cornmeal; place the dough seamside down on the towel and dust with flour. Cover the dough with a cotton towel and let rise 1 to 2 hours at room temperature until more than doubled in size.

Preheat oven to 450 to 500 degrees. Place the pot in the oven at least 30 minutes prior to baking to preheat. Once the dough has more than doubled in volume, remove the pot from the oven and place the dough in the pot seamside up. Cover with the lid and bake 30 minutes. Then remove the lid and bake 15 to 30 minutes uncovered, until the loaf is nicely browned.

Cool on a wire rack.

MAKES: 1 loaf

come to the table

This is what I want you to do: I want you to tell someone you love them, and dinner's at six. I want you to throw open your front door and welcome the people you love into the inevitable mess with hugs and laughter. I want you to light a burner on the stove, to chop and stir and season with love and abandon. Begin with an onion and a drizzle of olive oil, and go from there, any one of a million different places, any one of a million different meals.

Gather the people you love around your table and feed them with love and honesty and creativity. Feed them with your hands and the flavors and smells that remind you of home and beauty and the best stories you've ever heard, the best stories you've ever lived.

There will be a day when it all falls apart. My very dear friend lost her mom this year. That same month, another friend's marriage ended, shot through with lies and heartbreak. A friend I hadn't talked to in ages called late one Sunday night to ask me how to get through a miscarriage. "The bleeding," she said, "has already begun." As I write, a dear family friend lies in a coma in a hospital bed.

These are things I can't change. Not one of them. Can't fix, can't heal, can't put the broken pieces back together. But what I can do is offer myself, wholehearted and present, to walk with the people I love through the fear and the mess. That's all any of us can do. That's what we're here for.

Not the battle lines, keeping people in and out. Not the "pro" and "anti" stances, but the presence, the listening, the praying with and for on the days when it all falls apart, when life shatters in our hands.

The table is where we store up for those days, where we log minutes and hours building something durable and strong that gets tested in those terrible split seconds. And the table is where we return to stitch our hearts back together after the breaking.

I want you to stop running from thing to thing to thing, and to sit down at the table, to offer the people you love something humble and nourishing, like soup and bread, like a story, like a hand holding another hand while you pray. We live in a world that values us for how fast we go, for how much we accomplish, for how much life we can pack into one day. But I'm coming to believe it's in the in-between spaces that our lives change, and that the real beauty lies there.

Most of the time, I eat like someone's about to steal my plate, like I can't be bothered to chew or taste or feel, but I'm coming to see that the table is about food, and it's also about time. It's about showing up in person, a whole and present person, instead of a fragmented, frantic person, phone in one hand and to-do list in the other. Put them down, both of them, twin symbols of the modern age, and pick up a knife and a fork. The table is where time stops. It's where we look people in the eye, where we tell the truth about how hard it is, where we make space to listen to the whole story, not the textable sound bite.

They say the way to a man's heart is through his stomach. I believe that's absolutely true. Not that the way to land a guy is by baking him cookies, although it never hurts. But that if you can satiate a person's hunger, you can get a glimpse of their heart. There's an intimacy in it, in the meeting of needs and the filling of one's stomach, that is, necessarily, tied to the heart.

I want you to gobble life up in huge bites, tasting everything, trying every new flavor, remembering every smell and texture like it's the best thing you've ever had. I want you to live with wild and gorgeous abandon, throwing yourself into each day, telling the truth about who you are and who you are not, writing a love song to the world itself and to the God who made every inch of it.

I want you to invest yourself wholly and deeply in friendship, God's greatest evidence of himself here on earth. More than anything, I want you to come to the table. In all sorts of ways, both literally and metaphorically, come to the table.

We don't come to the table to fight or to defend. We don't come to prove or to conquer, to draw lines in the sand or to stir up trouble. We come to the table because our hunger brings us there. We come with a need, with fragility, with an admission of our humanity. The table is the great equalizer, the level playing field many of us have been looking everywhere for. The table is the place where the doing stops, the trying stops, the masks are removed, and we allow ourselves to be nourished, like children. We allow someone else to meet our need. In a world that prides people on not having needs, on going longer and faster, on going without, on powering through, the table is a place of safety and rest and humanity, where we are allowed to be as fragile as we feel. If the home is a body, the table is the heart, the beating center, the sustainer of life and health.

Come to the table.

appendix

I love you like a fat kid loves cake.

50 CENT

four-week book club/ cooking club discussion guide

Bread & Wine is divided into four parts, so you can invite a group of friends (or your small group or book club or supper club) to go through this Four-Week Book Club/Cooking Club Discussion Guide. Each week you can read and talk about one section, and you can also cook a few recipes from that section.

So gather your group, pick a night, and decide who's making what. The goal is that this guide starts good conversations, nudges you into the kitchen with a few new recipes, and helps you create some rich memories around the table with people you love.

Week One

1. In "My Mom's Blueberry Crisp," Shauna tells us about her food memories and the foods served around her family's table when she was growing up. What are some of your memories from your family's table during your childhood?

2. Whom do you think of when you hear Shauna talk about "her people"? Who are your people? How did they come to play that role in your life?

3. In "Enough," Shauna writes about longing for another child. Have you ever longed for something? What helped you through that season of longing?

4. Shauna writes about paying attention to the things that make you cry in "Run." What makes you cry? What might those tears mean for your future?

Week Two

1. In "Delicious Everywhere," Shauna writes about the tastes and flavors of places she's visited. What are some of the tastes and flavors you remember from places you've visited?

2. In "Jazz and Curry," Shauna writes about Thomas Keller's advice to make a recipe your own by making it three times. Are you a recipe user? Why or why not? What recipes from this book are you most looking forward to making your own?

3. In "Open the Door," Shauna writes that most women experience shame about their bodies and their homes. Is that true for you? What has helped you through that shame?

4. Shauna writes about trying to care for a friend but getting it wrong in "Cupcake in the Oven." Have you ever gotten it wrong? Or has a friend gotten it wrong when trying to care for you? What happened? What did you learn about yourself or about your friend?

Week Three

1. "Hail Mary" is about fear and about choosing to release fear and embrace faith and prayer. Have you experienced fear that threatened to take over? How did you choose faith instead?

2. In what area of your life do you most need the phrase "present over perfect"?

3. "The Bass Player's Birthday" is about birthday traditions. What are the meaningful birthday traditions your friends or family practice?

4. In "Swimming in Silence," Shauna unwittingly takes a trip without technology and learns about how important it is to be unplugged sometimes. How can you apply this concept to your own life?

Week Four

1. The Cooking Club hosts a garage sale and bake sale to benefit a food bank in "What Money Can't Buy." What are some similar ways you could live with less and give to a cause you believe in?

2. "Last-Minute Lunch Party" is about using what you have on hand for a last-minute party. What are your go-to recipes or dishes that you always make for a last-minute party? What are the recipes that make you think of your friends and family around your table?

3. "Swimsuit, Ready or Not" is about not waiting until we feel perfectly confident about our bodies to enjoy our lives. Have you ever found yourself hiding or waiting? What helped you out of that place?

4. In "Take This Bread," Shauna writes about the ways she's experienced the sacrament of Communion, both inside the church and outside of it. Share about your experiences of Communion, or your thoughts on its meaning and significance.

four-week book club/ cooking club menus

Part One

1. Green Salad with Basic Vinaigrette
2. Steak au Poivre with Cognac Pan Sauce
3. Basic Risotto
4. Blueberry Crisp

Part Two

1. Goat Cheese Biscuits
2. Green Well Salad
3. Mango Chicken Curry over rice
4. Nigella's Flourless Chocolate Brownies

Part Three

1. Bacon-Wrapped Dates
2. Watermelon Feta Salad
3. Magical White Bean Soup
4. Dark Chocolate Sea Salted Toffee with vanilla ice cream

Part Four

1. Brannon's Caesar Salad
2. Sweet Potato Fries with Sriracha Dipping Sauce
3. Mar-a-Lago Turkey Burgers
4. Gaia Cookies

on weeknight cooking, with pantry list

My friend Margaret came over to take a walk with me one evening, one of those great last-minute stopovers that makes an otherwise dreary day feel rich and lovely. We talked about a million things— writing, marriage, babies, creativity, storytelling, friendship, dinner. Margaret is a fantastic baker, more patient and precise than I'll ever be. As we walked, she said, "This is the thing: I can take three hours to bake and frost a cake on a Saturday afternoon, but on an average Tuesday night, Blaine and I just stare at each other, like, 'What's the plan?' "

In almost every part of life, the important moments are not the ones you'd think are the important ones. The really important moments are *before* the "big" moments. When you're writing, the moment you sit down at the keyboard isn't the magic moment; the magic moments are when you decide to see and hear and remember and taste everything in the whole world, choosing to believe that art and creativity are all around you, unfolding and beckoning you. And running is about sleep, water, getting a babysitter, not having that last glass or two of wine. By the time you've laced up your shoes and you're moving your feet, most of the hard choices have been made.

And the same is true when it comes to dinner. When I first

began to cook, I was a party cook. A weekend cook. I first learned how to make complicated meals with every bowl and pan in the kitchen, cookbook splashed with wine, sugar crunching underfoot, sixty-seven ingredients spread over every surface. But when it came to feeding Aaron and myself on the average weeknight, we were back to crackers and cheese or hummus and pita. Aaron would look forward to parties because at least then he was guaranteed a real home-cooked meal.

In recent years, though, I've become determined to master the weeknight dinner—rushed, no frills, no guests. Our little family, our table, cluttered with laptops and school projects, Batman guys, cables of every variety, sunglasses, and to-do lists.

It's a little bit counterintuitive. You'd think anyone can do a Tuesday dinner, but, say, feeding twenty on Saturday night or baking a wedding cake takes real skill. But I find it's exactly the opposite. That weeknight dinner takes planning and skill, a dance of art and science, all the while battling the clock and the crankiness of the weeknight dinner hour.

The weeknight dinner is largely about what you've already done, more so than what you do in that frantic six o'clock hour. What I mean is that planning and shopping are necessary parts of the weeknight dinner. When you're doing weekend cooking, lazy and messy, you've got all the time in the world to experiment, or to forget the ginger and head back to the store or call a neighbor. But Tuesday at 6:00 p.m., we don't have that kind of time. What separates the easy, lovely dinner from those glassy-eyed, worn-down disaster nights is, in one word, the pantry.

I'm sure there's an app that lets you fill in your own set of staples, and then check when you need to replenish it, but for me, I hold a basic mental list of what we always need. If I were a more routine-oriented person, I'd shop once a week, say, on Mondays. But I'm potentially the least routine-oriented person on earth, and

I absolutely cannot persuade myself into adopting little patterns like that, helpful as they would be. So maybe I go to the store every five days, and then the next time, every ten days, and then while I'm at Target a few days later, I pick up oatmeal, almond milk, and cheese. But all the while, I'm working from that mental pantry, the Things We Need, for our basic weeknight crush.

In her fantastic cookbook *Dinner: A Love Story*, Jenny Rosenstrach tells a story that I find myself thinking about at dinnertime fairly often. A friend of Jenny's mother told her that when she didn't know what to cook for dinner, she should start by dicing and cooking an onion, and that by the time the onion began to soften and fill the air with its rich, luxurious smell, something would come to her. I think she's exactly right, and I recommend the practice.

I also read recently that upon walking into the kitchen to prepare dinner, you should always grab an apple and an orange to buy yourself time with little ones—tiny, darling, ticking time bombs of hunger. This is an important idea for me, because if I'm feeling too overwhelmed, I default to feeding each one of us separately, according to urgency, and allowing us to eat in front of the TV and laptops, having narrowly avoided disaster. That's not how I want to spend our evenings, but I'm embarrassed at how often it happens. Putting out a small, healthy snack for all of us to grab buys me a little time to make a plan.

On the most average, least inspired of nights, when there's no energy to putter and create, the first step is to peer into the fridge for possible leftovers to lead the way and to ask the question: big salad, soup, rice bowl, taco? Those are the four simplest, most basic, most manageable weeknight dinners around our house.

I know that pasta tends to be a weeknight staple—quick-cooking, kid-friendly, versatile. But since Aaron's gluten-free, and one can only eat so much rice or corn pasta without a profound longing for the real, white, flour-filled stuff, pasta's not in our rotation very often. Same with sandwiches, for the same reason. You have to really want whatever's in that sandwich to get over gluten-free bread, so mostly we don't do all the substitutions and replacements and instead focus on eating big salads, soup, rice bowl, or tacos, our four go-to weeknight standbys.

Whatever leftovers I do locate will lead the way. Is there cooked rice? Cooked chicken from last night? Bits of this or that vegetable? I save everything, even the tiniest bits, and I find that sometimes they're the difference—just a few slices of day-old pork tenderloin or a cup of rice or quinoa or some roasted vegetables can steer us on our way.

First go-to: big salad. When I say big, what I mean is that this is no plate of lightly dressed greens to be served alongside a hunk of meat or bowl of pasta. This salad is a main stage event, no side dishes necessary. My friend Ruth basically taught me everything I know about salads, and I think of her every time I make a salad that's colorful and beautiful and loaded with all sorts of things.

Around our house, a salad almost always starts with baby spinach. Then we add protein, something crunchy, dried or fresh fruit, cheese, and vinaigrette—for example, diced chicken, pecans, dried cherries, fresh blackberries, goat cheese, and maple balsamic vinaigrette. Or mixed greens, chicken, walnuts, pears, Parmesan, and white wine vinaigrette.

Second go-to: soup. Soup generally only needs a few things: aromatics—the aforementioned onion, garlic, possibly ginger —rice, chicken, vegetables, perhaps a can of tomatoes, and fresh herbs. There are, of course, a million ways to make chicken and rice soup, but the building blocks are onion, cooked chicken, rice, broth, salt, and pepper. From there, ginger, lime, cilantro, a splash of soy sauce? Or garlic, canned diced tomatoes, fresh rosemary, a splash of balsamic? A few handfuls of baby spinach or frozen peas are good, as are carrots and celery, or even a few potatoes, cubed. Carrots and potatoes, though, will increase your cooking time, so if speed is the name of the game, cooked chicken and cooked rice are your best pals for soup.

Third go-to: rice bowl. If there are no salad greens but we do have some kind of meat and some other vegetables, then we do a rice bowl. The first step is to start the brown rice, because it takes the longest to cook. I put the rice and water on a back burner before I do anything else.

Next step: vegetable. I'd always steamed broccoli, I think, and never been particularly excited about it, but then one winter I went to stay with my friend Sara for a writing retreat, and she roasted broccoli with lots of sea salt as an afternoon snack. She told me it would taste like french fries. I was skeptical, understandably. And then she was right—absolutely delicious french-fryish bites of broccoli. Since that trip, broccoli has been a permanent fixture on the grocery list, a once-a-week (or more!) dinner staple.

Earlier this year, my sisters-in-law and mother-in-law asked me to teach them a few new recipes. They were looking for simple weeknight dinners for their families. We made white chicken chili, pasta with bolognese, goat cheese scrambled eggs, roasted broccoli, and breakfast cookies.

The broccoli, obviously, is the least exciting item on that list, but after the eggs and before the cookies, we cut up one crown into bite-size pieces, tossed it with olive oil and sea salt, and put it into a 425-degree oven for 12 to 15 minutes, tossing once.

My sister-in-law Amy had been skeptical, just as I had been, but when she tasted it, she said, "This? This is a broccoli game changer!" That phrase has made its way into lots of our conversations since then, and the broccoli has made its way to several of their tables.

Once the rice is doing its thing and the broccoli is on its way in the oven and the onion has filled up the house with the smell of dinner and possibility, then it's chicken time. You can fire up the grill, or pull out the indoor grill pan, but more often than not, I panfry either chicken breasts or chicken sausages. Chicken sausages are fantastic weeknight food because they're generally fully cooked, which makes them quick, and they're packed with flavor, so you don't even need to think about a sauce. Brown rice, chicken sausages, broccoli—and dinner is done.

If you're panfrying chicken breasts, brown them on both sides, and then let them rest, covered by a sheet of foil. Into the same pan, dump your now-golden and softened onion, a spoonful of Dijon, a glug of white wine if it's open, or if not, a few tablespoons of broth. Let that mixture bubble and cook down into a quick pan sauce. To add richness, you can add a knob of butter, or a few tablespoons of heavy cream or whole milk, sort of a lazy version of the cognac pan sauce from the steak au poivre recipe, but I find that the onion/Dijon/wine or broth is a good light sauce to pour over each bowl of rice, sliced chicken, and broccoli.

Or you can top the bowl with a splash of soy sauce and a fat wedge of lime, and then sprinkle it with chopped peanuts and cilantro. Or you can stir pesto through the rice, or salsa, especially salsa verde. And if you didn't use your onion in a pan sauce, stir it through your rice, or plop a generous amount over the top of your rice bowl, maybe with a tiny bit of goat cheese or some sliced almonds. Or invest in the future—put the now-nearly-caramelized onion in the refrigerator for tomorrow, and revel in the smell that lingers anyway.

There are nights, of course, when there just isn't a vegetable to be found, or when the freezer supply of chicken has been depleted. Enter canned beans. Throw a can of black beans into the rice with a spoonful of fresh salsa and some chopped cilantro. Or add white beans to rice and tomatoes and lots of rosemary, and then a serious glug of the best balsamic you have.

Fourth go-to: tacos. If waiting for rice to boil and cook is more than you can manage, my last-ditch effort at dinner is tacos: scrambled egg tacos, black bean and goat cheese tacos, sliced avocado and hummus tacos with a spoonful of salsa over the top. While I warm small corn tortillas between damp paper towels in the microwave, I forage for leftovers, and if the fridge is truly bare, I open a can of black beans and warm them with a spoonful of barbecue sauce.

Pantry List

In terms of a pantry, a weeknight, plain old, not-entertaining-but-just-feeding-the-family pantry, this is what I try to keep on hand. And this is a dinner-minded pantry—there are other things we keep around for breakfast and baking, of course. But if we have these things, no matter the chaos of the day, what we know is that there will be dinner.

Weeknight Dinner Pantry

> Brown rice
> Canned black beans
> Canned white beans
> Canned diced tomatoes
> Olive oil
> Balsamic vinegar
> Nuts (almonds, pecans, walnuts, peanuts)
> Dried fruit (cherries, cranberries, figs, raisins)
> Chicken broth
> Onions

Weeknight Dinner Freezer

Chicken breasts
Chicken sausages
Fresh ginger, wrapped well
Parmesan cheese, not grated
Frozen peas

Weeknight Dinner Refrigerator

Corn tortillas
Eggs
Baby spinach
Broccoli
Carrots
Celery
Apples
Goat cheese
Feta cheese
Soy sauce
Dijon
Lime
Lemon
Cilantro
Rosemary
Basil
Butter

my best entertaining tips, with sample menus

My friend Becky was hosting her first big party, and she sent me an email looking for some direction. This is what I sent back to her. These are, in my opinion, the most important things to keep in mind when you're entertaining.

1. Find a way to entertain that works for you.
It doesn't have to be spectacular. There's no one right way. Hospitality is about love, not about performance. Above all else, people want to feel welcomed by someone who wants them in their home. No matter how unimpressive the food is or how messy the house is, if you greet your guests at the door with happiness and warmth, they'll feel glad they came.

And, of course, at the same time, the food can be flawless and the napkins fashioned into origami, but if the host is so nervous it's clear she's counting the minutes till you leave, nothing can save that party. As a host, you set the tone, and you set it right away. It's so easy to get carried away with an ambitious menu, and then spend the whole night flinging things around your kitchen and being annoyed with your guests for having the audacity to try to talk with you. Terrible plan. Everyone would rather have a simpler meal and a happier host.

Every entertaining decision you make should be based on the goal of "happy, relaxed host." It should guide the guest list, the menu, the décor—how much can you do and still be a happy and relaxed host?

Some people love open houses and buffets but stress out about seated dinner parties. Some people like cocktail parties but don't want to do a whole meal. My friend Heather hosts a formal afternoon tea every Christmas because she loves to bake and loves an excuse to use her china. I'm a dinner party girl: I like six to twelve people around the table, with homey, unfussy food. Find what works for you, and stick with that.

2. When the doorbell rings, have yourself ready, music on, something to eat, something to drink.

I think it's totally OK to have the food undone, as long as there's music and candles, and the host is ready. It's not OK to come to the door in a towel, even if the food is ready. If when the first person arrives you're ready, the music is on, and the candles are lit, no problem. But if your hair is wet and it's dead silent, even if the food is done, that makes people feel like you're not ready for them. If there's a time crunch, leave the food till the last minutes. No one minds helping in the kitchen, but it's no fun to leave them in the living room while you put on makeup.

I make sure the music, candles, appetizers, and wine are all set and I'm all ready, and sometimes I even leave a few cooking things undone so people can help me in the kitchen. Shy people especially often love having a job to do.

3. Be prepared and make a detailed plan.

In most areas of my life I'm a sort of laid-back, messy, chaotic person. But when it comes to a dinner party, I've got lists and charts and Post-its everywhere. I wake up in the middle of the

night and think about salad plates or the best way to serve—
buffet or family-style.

What allows me to be a happy, relaxed host is planning. It
doesn't mean you won't forget anything—it means you'll have
time to fix whatever you've forgotten. One thing that always
used to trip me up is timing. I'd run into a traffic jam about thirty
minutes before we were supposed to eat, and I'd realize, all at
once, that I needed more hands, more burners, and more oven
space *right then*. This sounds so fussy, but I like to map out all
the recipes, cooking times, burners, and oven space, and then
lay everything out—every ingredient, every chair, every platter.

When that's done, I shower and get dressed, and then I do
all the cooking. When I'm making the plan for the day, working
backward, I allow myself at least 30 minutes to putter around
lighting candles, putting on music, putting on lipstick, having
a glass of wine.

**4. Develop a repertoire and make only one last-minute
dish per meal.**

I like living on the edge, so I frequently try new recipes for
parties. I don't really recommend this. Pick a few recipes and
get really comfortable with them, so at least that part of it is
stress-free. People would much rather have a meal they've had
at your house before than deal with a stressed-out host. And I
think people remember through flavors, and that's a good thing.
Cassoulet always makes me think of my mom, and Annette's
enchiladas, of course, always remind me of her, even though she
lives across the country. Develop a little repertoire of meals that
people who gather around your table will come to expect and
look forward to.

If the entertaining and hosting part is intimidating for you,
keep the menu really, really simple. Choose an appetizer that can

be prepped early, an entrée that can be in the oven when guests are arriving, easy salad and bread, and a dessert that's already prepared. A heavy, yummy entrée like lasagna or enchiladas feels homey in a good way, and it doesn't need much else.

5. Accept help. Let people bring things, help you cook, clean up—again, it's not a performance.

People love to help. Some people will offer, and some will even just jump up and start setting the table or refilling drinks, but no one minds being asked. At my parents' cottage, the rule is that because the women generally cook, the men always do the dishes and cleanup. It doesn't matter if it's your first dinner there or your hundredth—when dinner is over, the women refill their wine glasses and retire to the porch, and the men set up an assembly line from the table to the sink.

When people are arriving, ask someone to make sure the other guests have drinks, and ask someone else to slice bread, toss salad, or set the table. Make sure they have everything they need, and then let them have at it. Some people will have a million questions about how to do it exactly perfectly, and some will take a job and run, but either way, they feel included right off the bat —and that's so much better than sitting alone in an empty living room while all the action and the good smells are in the kitchen.

When people offer to bring something, always say yes, and be as specific as you can without crossing over into massively annoying. One note: only ask someone to bring an appetizer or cocktail if you know for sure they're early arrivers. I hate opening the door to guests and knowing that delicious tamales and margaritas are on their way, but in the meantime, all I have out are napkins. I try to do the main course, the appetizer, and the first couple bottles of wine, and then the rest I'm happy to let people fill in.

Assorted other thoughts. Light a candle, but not a hundred of them. I do like what one candle does, or two, in separate spaces, but when I walk into someone's house and they've got eighty-seven candles lit, each with a different scent, I wonder if maybe I'm in the wrong place, and if someone's getting engaged.

On the topic of the actual table: you may imagine I'm all table-scape-y, but I'm decidedly not. For me, it's about the gathering, not the table settings, and I find that people feel a little uptight when the table looks like a woodland village or something. I always, always use white plates, and all my other stuff is wood and silver so I can switch things up with napkins or candles or place cards. And even though I have that option, 90 percent of the time I use white tapers in silver candlesticks and a low bowl of white hydrangeas. Simple, clean, warm, homey.

Again, the point is to gather people you love around your table often enough for them to feel comfortable there. If I had to build a Rose Parade float for a centerpiece every time I have people over, I'd never have people over, and that's the heart of the conversation —what works for you, in your house, with your schedule, with your gifts and budget and preferences.

I have white dishes, lots and lots of them, and they're cheap, because I never want to be brokenhearted when something breaks. Same with glassware. We have very pretty three-dollar wine glasses, and I'm so glad we do, because when someone inevitably knocks one over, I love being able to tell them that really, really it's not a big deal. Because that's one of the highest values in our home: safety. I want to have a home where people feel like they can rest—like they can wear slippers, get themselves a glass of water, settle in for an evening.

It's about what works for your guests, your family, the people you love and have welcomed around your table. It's not about what will look great on Pinterest or Instagram later. It's about loving the people in your life by gathering them close into the private space of your home, about giving them soft places to land in hard seasons, about meeting their needs for food, for listening, for peace, for rest.

Sample Menus for Entertaining

Summer Dinner Party

    Watermelon Feta Salad
    Esquites
    Mar-a-Lago Turkey Burgers
    Blueberry Crisp with vanilla ice cream

Cozy Fall Party

    Sullivan Street Bread with sharp cheddar and Dijon
    Green Well Salad
    Real Simple Cassoulet
    Gaia Cookies

Fancy Winter Dinner Party

    Bacon-Wrapped Dates
    Steak au Poivre with Cognac Pan Sauce
    Basic Risotto
    Simplest Dark Chocolate Mousse

Springtime Lunch Party

    Maple Balsamic Pork Tenderloin
    Farmers Market Potato Salad
    Brannon's Caesar Salad
    Nigella's Flourless Chocolate Brownies

Fiesta

Chips, salsa, guacamole (avocadoes, jalapeños, onion, cilantro,
   lime, salt)
Annette's Enchiladas
Esquites
Black beans warmed in a cast-iron pan with a few tablespoons
   of barbecue sauce
Dark Chocolate Sea Salted Toffee with vanilla ice cream

recommended reading

Favorite Food Writing

Tender at the Bone and *Comfort Me with Apples* by Ruth Reichl
A Homemade Life by Molly Wizenberg
Supper of the Lamb by Father Robert Farrar Capon
An Everlasting Meal by Tamar Adler
Animal, Vegetable, Miracle by Barbara Kingsolver
Blood, Bones & Butter by Gabrielle Hamilton
Home Cooking by Laurie Colwin

Favorite Cookbooks

Feast and *How to Eat* by Nigella Lawson
The Barefoot Contessa Cookbook and *Barefoot in Paris*
    by Ina Garten
Dinner: A Love Story by Jenny Rosenstrach
How to Cook Everything by Mark Bittman
In the Kitchen with a Good Appetite by Melissa Clark
The Smitten Kitchen Cookbook by Deb Perelman

Favorite Memoirs and Writing on Faith and Life

Traveling Mercies by Anne Lamott
A Million Miles in a Thousand Years by Donald Miller
Take This Bread by Sara Miles
Still by Lauren Winner
Jesus, My Father, the CIA, and Me by Ian Morgan Cron
Nice Girls Don't Change the World by Lynne Hybels
I Thought It Was Just Me and *Daring Greatly* by Brené Brown

recipe index

recipe index
by category

acknowledgments

One of the greatest joys of my writing life is working with two wise and loving editors, Angela Scheff and Carolyn McCready, who have become dear friends along the way. Many thanks to my agent and friend Chris Ferebee, and to the marketing team at Zondervan led by Londa Alderink. Thanks as well to Heather Adams and the truly fantastic Kelly Hughes. Thanks to Dirk Buursma for careful and elegant copyediting; to Lindsay Sherbondy for her lovely lettering; to Blaine Hogan, Bjorn Amundsen, and Rachel Reiman for their beautiful and creative work. Thanks times one billion to Brannon Anderson.

My parents, Bill and Lynne, and my in-laws, Dan and Diane, take care of our boys with such love and tenderness, and Aaron and I couldn't work or travel the way we do without their help. Thanks and love to the friends who walk through life with us on the bright days and the dark ones: the Cooking Club, my brother Todd, Annette and Andrew Richards, Joe and Emily Hays, Steve and Sarah Carter, Matt and Kristi Lundgren, Brian and Jorie Johnson, Jimmy and Leanne Mellado, Ryan and Emily Gardner.

One million hugs and thanks to the friends and family who read early versions of the manuscript and offered helpful and wise feedback along the way, including several of the people listed above, and also dear friends Monica Robertson, Laura Tremaine,

Laura Turner, September Vaudrey, Heather Larson, Margaret Feinberg, Amy Fannin, Brittany Niequist, and Emily Sinke.

Thanks and love from our kitchen to the chefs, cooks, and cookbook writers who have taught me along the way and whose recipes I included and/or adapted for this book: Nigella Lawson, Art Smith and Table Fifty-Two, Jim Lahey and the Sullivan Street Bakery, Ina Garten, Heidi Swanson from 101 Cookbooks, Nancy Silverton, Sally Sampson, Grace Parisi, The Green Well, Gaia, The Chopping Block, *Food & Wine*, *Bon Appetit*, *Real Simple*, and *O, The Oprah Magazine*.

Thanks to Anne Lamott and Brené Brown, for writing books that put words to how I want to live.

Many thanks to Shalise Hickman, Julie Grissom, Michelle Panek, Sarah Mennie, and the rest of the fantastic PromiseTowne team.

Thanks and much love to the recipe testers who opened their kitchens to these stories and flavors and recipes, who gave great feedback and encouragement and suggestions: Kristin Smith, Amy Flesher, Abby Manchesky, Nina Gardner, Jessica Brazeal, Shelly Carlson, Sarah Harmeyer, Carrie Cox, Amanda Leatherman, Betsy Fallon, Emily Stebila, Erica Ladd, Sarah McCabe, Bethany Suckrow, Christine Dumais, Kaitlin Jones, Robyn Devine, Cathy Delk, Kelly Kastens, Nicole Duprez, Joanna Kopp, Leslie Shogren, Lindsey Adams, Shannon Carter, Leah Fruth, Sarah Baar, Caitlin Leimbach, Crystal Calkins, Brittany Adcock, Christine Gough, Kaytee Bute, Mindi Wood, Ashley Vaughan, Julie Eckert, Rebecca Rohrscheib, Becca Sandahl, Hana Price, Hannah Schaefer, Laura Sartell, Brittany D. Judy, Lauren Hebel, Mike Calia, Monica Gee, Ashley Ford, Haley Burress, Lauren Shaw, Priscilla Peters, Addie Boone, Emily Macrane, Melissa Horton, Caitlin Bristow, Jen Bradbury, Jackie Rice, Jessica Holli, Samantha Johnson, Sarah Lubach, Alexandra Pinkus, Katie Howard, Kristin Littrell, Sara McDonald, Brittany Thurman, Kat Vinson, Belinda Bauman, Donna Bucholtz, Jennifer

Green, Amanda Blackburn, Kelsey N. Hutcheson, Laura Pearse, Melissa Larkin, Amanda Kemmeling-Fleshood, Laura Murray, Lauren Wojcik, Alissa Goudswaard, Lindsey Bandy, Sheila Johnson, Suzanne McKay, Natalie Farthing, Patti Snyder, Heather Yanke-Lunneberg, Carrie Jones, Tracy Bradford, Amy Simpson, Anika Swensen, Ashley Tuite, Jennifer Bowman, Dawn Bryant, Elizabeth Parnell, Kristina Wait, Lauren Hogan, Megan Kimmelshue, Dana Shultz, Jay & Katherine Wolf, Sarah Beckler, Sherrine Francis, Amanda Joy Stephen, Julianna & Tom Pryor, Donna Landwehr, Emilee Hurlbert, Leigh Kramer, Shannon Whitmer, Alanna Cathcart, Sarah Downey, Letha Gillisse, Lori Bailey, Molly Brown, Parker Vander Ploeg.

And I'll end the same way I began—with great love and deep gratitude for the three boys in my life, Aaron, Henry, and Mac. I'm so thankful that your three faces are the ones I get to see, day in and day out, around our table.

Cold Tangerines

Celebrating the Extraordinary Nature of Everyday Life

Shauna Niequist

Cold Tangerines — now available in softcover — is a collection of stories that celebrate the extraordinary moments hidden in your everyday life. It is about God, and about life, and about the thousands of daily ways in which an awareness of God changes and infuses everything. It is about spiritual life, and about all the things that are called nonspiritual life that might be spiritual after all. It is the snapshots of a young woman making peace with herself and trying to craft a life that captures the energy and exuberance we all long for in the midst of the fear and regret and envy we all carry with us. It is both a voice of challenge and song of comfort, calling you upward to the best possible life and giving you room to breathe, to rest, to break down and break through.

Cold Tangerines offers bright and varied glimpses of hope and redemption, in and among the heartbreak and boredom and broken glass.

Available in stores and online!

ZONDERVAN®
.com